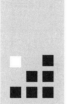

Collaborative
THEME BUILDING

Related Titles

Collaborative THEME BUILDING

How Teachers Write Integrated Curriculum

Dorothy M. Campbell
California University of Pennsylvania

Linda S. Harris

Allyn and Bacon
Boston ■ London ■ Toronto ■ Sydney ■ Tokyo ■ Singapore

Series editor: Traci Mueller
Series editorial assistant: Bridget Keane
Marketing manager: Stephen Smith

Library of Congress Cataloging-in-Publication Data

Campbell, Dorothy M.
    Collaborative theme building : how teachers write integrated curriculum /
Dorothy M. Campbell, Linda S. Harris
        p. cm.
    Includes bibliographical references and index.
    ISBN 0-205-32354-5
    1. Teacher participation in curriculum planning.   2. Interdisciplinary approach
in education.   I. Harris, Linda S.   II. Title.

LB2806.15 .C33 2001
375'.001—dc21

00-059413

Printed in the United States of America
10 9 8 7 6 5 4 3 2 1   04 03 02 01 00

Contents

Preface

OVERVIEW

Children come to school believing that learning is magic. Teachers, too, believe that learning can be relevant and exciting. They are searching for curriculum options that will translate these beliefs into reality in their classrooms. Many have found thematic teaching to be one option which allows students and teachers to rediscover the magic in learning. In an integrated thematic curriculum, "finding out" matters. Reading, writing, noticing, investigating, and understanding become exciting. Furthermore, the integration of disciplines is one way teachers can cope with the explosion of information and the overcrowded curriculum. The ultimate goal of theme work is that students achieve in-depth understanding as well as positive dispositions toward inquiry so they become enthusiastic lifelong learners. Classroom teachers bring this learning potential to life; therefore, it is they who make the best curriculum builders. Interdisciplinary curriculum makes such good sense to teachers that the question no longer is "Should we integrate the disciplines?" but "How can we do it with excellence and efficiency?"

Interdisciplinary thematic curriculum development is a creative, demanding, and open-ended process. Planning theme studies can seem overwhelming for teachers because so many possibilities exist. Often, valuable time is wasted during curriculum development because teachers are not confident about exactly how to proceed. This book presents a workable step-by-step curriculum writing model that bridges the gap between theory and practice, beginning with choosing a theme focus and ending with the completion of the ultimate thematic curriculum resource, a Theme Box. This model is unique in that it clearly delineates the role of the curriculum writing team from the role of the teacher implementing the theme studies. This practical book also describes effective collaborative team-building procedures. Collaboration builds creative synergy and overcomes isolation in the teaching profession. Because the collaborative aspect of thematic curriculum development is critical to success, this book explores ways to build a school-based team and use team mechanics. Without sacrificing creativity, our model is designed to help teams efficiently meet the challenging task of designing integrated thematic curriculum.

AUDIENCE

This book is intended for both preservice and inservice teachers wanting to develop integrated thematic curriculum. Inservice teachers charged with this responsibility will welcome the practical assistance this book provides. Likewise, principals and curriculum specialists will find this book helpful in leading school-based curriculum development efforts. Although the examples and experiences cited in this book primarily come from the elementary level, educators writing thematic curriculum from preschool through university levels will find our process valuable. The concepts are adaptable to any educational level. Even preservice teachers writing their first theme studies experience success with our detailed step-by-step procedures.

UNIQUE FEATURES

Team-Building Tools

When developing a curriculum, teachers can maximize creativity and productivity by collaborating on school-based writing teams. Although such collaboration is universally advocated, very few authors offer direct help with the team development processes and skills that are presented in this book. Furthermore, we present the cycle of change teachers can expect to experience as they develop into cohesive teams. Team-building skills such as coordinating work styles, building consensus, sharing work assignments, and brainstorming are explored.

Options

Many books on thematic curriculum design or interdisciplinary teaching advocate specific types of theme hubs, teaching approaches, or assessment options. Our book clarifies the many choices in these and other areas, thus allowing teams to make decisions based on their specific strengths and needs. We present numerous options in team organization, such as choices in team composition, team role assignments, and team mechanics. Choices in the curriculum development processes include multiple ways of identifying the theme parameters, various approaches to gathering and organizing information, and alternate strategies for assessing student learning. This book also clarifies product options. Each Theme Box will be unique as teams make choices, beginning with the theme focus and ending with the supplemental resources to be included.

The Theme Box

The most valuable product a curriculum writing team can generate is what we refer to as the Theme Box. The Theme Box is a resource collection that includes essential concepts and questions, assessment options, activity ideas, background information, supporting teaching materials, student products, and selected pieces of theme-related literature. The Theme Box preserves the work of the team and provides a substantial, flexible resource for the entire school. Unlike a teaching unit designed to be used by one teacher or one team at one grade level, the Theme Box is a resource unit that can be adapted and used by various teachers at various grade levels throughout the school or district. Thus, the Theme Box is a practical solution for maximizing the value of the time invested by the curriculum writing team.

Action Pack

This book includes an Action Pack of work organizers providing step-by-step procedures for curriculum development. Unlike typical training exercises or simulations, the Action Pack pages guide teams through the actual tasks involved in writing integrated thematic studies. Purposeful and valuable in the real world of curriculum writing, they provide structure that fosters both creativity and productivity. The Action Pack allows even first-time teams to be successful. Through Action Pack field testing with both preservice and inservice teachers, we have eliminated busy work and included only the most helpful work organizers. Clearly, different teams have found different pages to be useful in different ways. Your team should select those pages most applicable to your situation and suited to your objectives. Some pages will prompt discussion; others may require several copies for team members to use for written documentation; a few pages may be deemed unnecessary for your team. When introducing each specific task in the theme building and team building processes, we refer you to the Action Pack pages that will help you to perform and document that task. Using the Action Pack in concert with the text, your curriculum writing team can successfully and confidently create exciting integrated thematic curriculum.

ADDITIONAL FEATURES

Each chapter begins with guiding questions that provide focus and serve as advance organizers for chapter content. Guiding questions are central to our theme development model. We use them in this book to demonstrate their value and use. Your team may choose to write guiding questions to focus theme studies for your students.

We have drawn samples of curriculum writing products from the work of preservice and inservice elementary teachers. These appear throughout the book as each new phase of theme-building is introduced. In addition, we have provided rubrics and criteria lists to help your team evaluate your evolving theme study. We use graphic organizers extensively to summarize major ideas and recommendations. To avoid the cumbersome use of the phrase "he or she," we have alternated the use of pronouns when referring to preservice and inservice teachers.

FIELD TESTING

The ideas in this book have been field tested with over 40 teams of both preservice undergraduate and graduate students as well as practicing teachers. These varied teams have written curriculum for themes of their choice. Our university library circulates the resulting Theme Boxes to student teachers and local elementary teachers, who use them to develop teaching units. All the teams involved have contributed to the methods described in this model. They have approached theme-building with a willingness to experiment, analyze, invent, and reflect. This has also included a few trips down some frustrating paths. Nevertheless, team members have invariably recommended this process to their colleagues. It works! We trust all future groups building upon the model will do so in the same spirit of openness and adventure.

Dorothy M. Campbell initiated this model of thematic curriculum development and the creation of Theme Boxes in a course she developed at California University of Pennsylvania. Discouraged by the lack of materials providing practical help with thematic resource units, she began writing a text for her students. Linda S. Harris was one of the graduate students enrolled in this thematic teaching class. While challenging Dorothy to provide more guidance on team development and skills, Linda soon found herself collaborating on this book. Linda's background as a team supervisor in the business world provided valuable insight into how curriculum writing teams might function more productively. Because they each offer a unique perspective, you will find personal anecdotes interspersed throughout this text, reflecting their experiences and thoughts.

Acknowledgments

This book is the result of learning from and with over forty curriculum writing teams, comprising both graduate and undergraduate students at California University of Pennsylvania. Thanks are due to every one of these theme builders, especially those who allowed us to use samples of their work and those who commented on early drafts of the manuscript for this book. Special thanks go to Susie Molish and her second graders who participated in field-testing a Theme Box on the African grass-lands.

We are especially indebted to Susan Gatti of Indiana University of Pennsylvania for her thoughtful and careful review of the manuscript.

Our appreciation goes to the following reviewers for their helpful comments on the manuscript: William S. Harwood, Indiana University, and Theresa Perez, University of North Carolina at Charlotte.

We have been supported in our work by numerous colleagues, friends, and family members. Among our biggest supporters have been Linda's parents, Richard and Beulah Harris, and Dorothy's daughters, Alicia, Alexandra, and Oressa. Dorothy's husband, Allan, deserves special thanks for the countless gourmet meals prepared to fuel our creativity.

Collaborative
THEME BUILDING

CHAPTER 1

Exploring Successful Theme Building

GUIDING QUESTIONS:

Why Do Teachers Value Integrated Theme Studies?
What Is Needed for Successful Theme Building?

KRISTINE'S JOURNAL

March 3

Today all the second grade teachers in the district got together for another meeting. At this meeting we were to plan a thematic unit on transportation. I was excited about this meeting because I thought I would finally have an idea of what we are expected to do in our classrooms. How wrong I was.

March 20

It has been great to have planning time every week with the other second grade teachers in my building. When I started teaching last year, I benefited from the wonderful things I learned from these experienced teachers. Last Wednesday we did our plans together again. We talked more about integrating our curriculum but nothing specific seems to get planned. It seems hard to integrate all of our subjects around a theme and find the time to plan it.

June 1

Today was another disappointing day at a district-wide meeting on curricular issues. Sometimes all this talk about change seems foolhardy. Everyone wants it until the opportunity presents itself. . . . As a new teacher, I hear so much dissatisfaction with the way things are, but I'm not sure that people really know how to change. It is all so frustrating.

The above excerpts are from a journal kept by Kristine during her second year as a teacher. In its entirety, Kristine's journal is a portrait of a busy, motivated teacher with multiple roles to fill, wide-ranging responsibilities to meet, and numerous goals to accomplish. However, uppermost in the mind of Kristine, and indeed in the minds of most teachers, is one goal: to teach students valuable, relevant content in a way that facilitates understanding and motivation. To achieve this goal, teachers need an overall plan. This overall plan for what is taught and when it is taught is called curriculum.

Kristine was asked by her school district to fill a new role—curriculum writer—while creating a new kind of product: integrated thematic curriculum. Integrated thematic curriculum organizes content around a central focus, such as a topic or problem, and then develops the most important aspects of the focus by freely crossing discipline lines.

Dissatisfied with the status quo in their classrooms and schools, teachers around the country are undertaking curriculum writing endeavors similar to Kristine's. Unfortunately, many teachers' experiences resemble Kristine's in another respect: as they create this curriculum, teachers often feel as if they are on a roller coaster ride, with high points of excitement and hope and low points of doubt and discouragement. Clearly, Kristine's journal ends on one of those low points. After three months with no visible progress toward a new curriculum, Kristine was questioning the teachers' abilities to change.

Kristine and her co-teachers were enthusiastic, motivated, committed teachers who wanted to change their curriculum to better meet their students' needs. In spite of this, they failed to make significant progress in the three-month period chronicled in the journal because they lacked some key ingredients essential to successful theme building. This book is written for Kristine, her more experienced colleagues, and countless other teachers who want to work toward a more integrated curriculum but are not sure exactly how to proceed. It is also written for preservice teachers who will be expected to know how to write integrated curriculum and function well on curriculum teams. By following the workable step-by-step model for curriculum writing presented in this book, teachers can successfully build integrated thematic curriculum.

However, before exploring in depth how to build integrated theme studies, you need to understand why in recent years so many teachers have chosen to move toward curriculum integration.

WHY DO TEACHERS VALUE INTEGRATED THEME STUDIES?

Understanding integrated thematic studies begins with exploring both traditional and integrated curriculum options. The value of integrated thematic curriculum cannot be grasped without understanding how it differs from traditional curriculum.

Traditional Curriculum Options

Traditionally, American educators have based their curricular decisions on the assumption that students learn best when the content is broken down into small steps and separated into logical subdivisions. Thus, most schools have organized their curriculum by compartmentalizing it into separate subjects or disciplines. Reading skills are developed during a block of time called reading; math skills are assigned a distinct time slot called math; and science is taught independently from social studies. Within each school subject, content has been broken down further into small logical steps. For the most part, the writing of such curriculum has been left entirely to curriculum specialists and textbook authors. To achieve delineation of the steps for a complex skill, a curriculum developer does a task analysis, identifying the beginning subskills. Then the curriculum specialist builds logically from the simplest subskill up to the complex skill. To practice the prerequisite subskills, learners are often required to repeat contrived tasks on worksheets. Real-world tasks, such as writing paragraphs or stories, are delayed until subskills are mastered. If the content is informational in nature, the curriculum developer designs content coverage that moves logically from simpler ideas to more complex ones, building precept upon precept. Such content typically has been presented in carefully sequenced textbooks. This "take apart" approach to curriculum has its roots in the behaviorist school of thought. B. F. Skinner, a leading behaviorist, advocated three requirements for effective curriculum: (1) information is presented in small increments or steps, (2) immediate feedback is provided to learners, and (3) self-pacing through the steps is implemented (Hergenhahn & Olson, 1997).

Integrated Curriculum Options

Now more than ever before, American educators are challenging the basic assumption that understanding is easiest to achieve when broken down or taken apart. They advocate just the opposite, maintaining that knowledge is best achieved when tasks are complex, with ideas interconnected rather than separated. Many of these educators are part of a school of thought called constructivism. Based principally on the ideas of Piaget (1954, 1963), Vygotsky (1962, 1978), and Dewey (1916, 1938), the constructivist philosophy posits that learners are always actively constructing their own knowledge by striving to make sense of their world. Primarily, students make sense by making connections among ideas as they integrate new experiences into their prior knowledge. The constructivist views the learner as competent and capable of dealing with complexities.

In the constructivist view, teachers can make knowledge and understanding more accessible to their students if they use curriculum that strengthens connections. Thus, to the constructivist, a new type of curriculum is needed: a connected or integrated curriculum that supports learners as they actively build knowledge. In an integrated, constructivist curriculum, learning typically starts with complex tasks significant in the learner's real world. For example, instead of practicing subskills on worksheets, kindergartners are invited to write stories "the way kindergarten children write," with pictures, some words, and invented spellings. Third graders learn researching skills through actual library investigations rather than through practice with a set of sequenced tasks in a simulated setting. Middle school students learn interpersonal and organizational skills, as well as content, as they work in teams to create and implement their own experimental designs, much as researchers of all kinds do in the real world.

Educators are searching for alternatives to the "take apart" curriculum on practical as well as philosophical grounds, as they face an increasingly overcrowded curriculum. Knowledge has grown astronomically, but the time in the classroom has remained the same. Much of this new knowledge is valuable and clearly deserves attention. Furthermore, to enable students to function well in society, parents, community groups, and governments have given the schools new priorities. Programs in drug awareness, AIDS prevention, personal safety, cultural pride, conflict resolution, and school and community cooperative learning are just a few of these. No longer can every new addition to the curriculum be given its own time allocation. As more is added to the curriculum, the danger increases that content coverage will become more and more superficial, preventing students from gaining a deep understanding of anything they learn. One effective way to deal with a bulging curriculum is an integrated approach. Many skills and many subjects can be effectively integrated into one interdisciplinary unit of study. In-depth study of a few content-rich topics is preferred over shallow coverage of several isolated topics.

Another problem with the traditional "take apart" approach to curriculum has been that of motivation. Students find it difficult to see the relevance of what they are studying when content is presented as discrete facts and isolated subskills within compartmentalized disciplines. They find it hard to imagine that they will ever need a particular skill or piece of information when they are not learning it within a meaningful context. If students are asked to master all the mechanics before engaging in the real-life aspects that can make learning magical, they may find the wait too long to sustain motivation and enthusiasm for school.

A connected or integrated curriculum holds promise for keeping students excited about learning and positive about school. When the curriculum is organized to convey how knowledge is connected to multiple disciplines and to real life, its relevance is more apparent to students. The content and value of their studies make more sense to the students. Figure 1.1 provides a comparative summary of the traditional and the integrated curricular approaches.

Figure 1.1   *Comparison of Traditional and Integrated Curriculum Approaches*

Traditional Curriculum Options	Integrated Curriculum Options
Learning is organized in small steps.	Learning stays connected and whole.
Learning moves from the simplest to the most complex ideas.	Learning starts with complex tasks.
Curriculum uses contrived activities, with tasks controlled to be focused on small increments.	Curriculum uses authentic activities with tasks as "real world" as possible.
Disciplines are treated separately.	Studies are interdisciplinary.
Ideas are developed in a tight, logical sequence.	Ideas are pursued differently as each student searches for meaning and understanding.
Skills are taught deliberately and in isolation. Complex skills are delayed until subskills have been learned.	Skills are taught deliberately when needed for authentic reasons.
The simplest ideas yielded by a task analysis most influence the beginning points of a curriculum.	Developmental stages, interests, and prior knowledge of students most influence the beginning points of a curriculum.
Single text is used, often with a controlled vocabulary.	Multiple resources are used, with natural vocabularies.
Students receive information.	Students are actively involved in searching for meaning.
Learning is self-paced.	Learning is self-directed.
Curriculum is typically taught to individual students and/or the entire class.	Curriculum is typically developed collaboratively in small groups.
Curriculum is teacher directed.	Curriculum is negotiated.

The Integrated Thematic Curriculum Option

Constructivist teachers can choose from a wide repertoire of options to integrate curriculum, including discovery learning, inquiry learning, the project approach, writing across the curriculum, independent research, real-life problem investigations, studies of various genres of literature, emergent curriculum, whole language curriculum, and any integration of separate but overlapping school subjects such as science and math. One of the most successful, popular, and exciting options for connecting learning has been integrated thematic teaching. Although Dewey and others in the Progressive Movement advocated integrated thematic teaching as early as the 1920s, only now is it widely practiced in American education. Integrated theme studies connect ways of learning and content from more than one discipline by organizing the curriculum around a central focus. The theme study provides relevant, in-depth study that enables learners to construct meaningful, lasting knowledge and transferable learning strategies.

Educators seeking to provide relevant, motivating curriculum through integrated theme studies agree that the best people to design this type of curriculum are not curriculum specialists, but teachers themselves. Teachers have the most current and accurate knowledge of their students and communities. They have the ability and the responsibility to evaluate state requirements and local curricular priorities in light of student needs. They are in an ideal position to determine natural connections in the curriculum they implement. Thus, more and more, classroom teachers are being called upon to fill the role of curriculum writers. While this role is exciting for teachers, many find that it can also be confusing, overwhelming, and frustrating at times. Teachers writing curriculum need support to be successful. They need the same key ingredients for success that would have helped Kristine and her colleagues.

WHAT IS NEEDED FOR SUCCESSFUL THEME BUILDING?

A look at the full text of Kristine's first journal entry will provide insights into the elements needed for successful theme building. On March 3, Kristine and her colleagues were struggling to understand their new task of curriculum development.

KRISTINE'S JOURNAL

March 3

At the district-wide meeting of second grade teachers, we began by breaking down transportation into air, land, and sea. Each group was to address a subtopic through various subjects: math, reading, dramatic play, etc. We brainstormed ideas and later presented them to the whole group. I found in working with my group that everyone was throwing out ideas, but each had a different perspective on what we were looking for. When each group presented its topic, everything was accepted and nothing seemed wrong. Afterward, I felt even further from knowing what was expected of me.

At lunch I found that I was not alone in my confusion. Most of these teachers had been teaching in the district for at least 20 years, but even they were unsure about what was expected of us. There seemed to be a fear among the older teachers who had been trained in curricular innovations before that the district would lose interest and eventually enthusiasm would fizzle and all this would be wasted time. When we came back from lunch, we saw a video of classrooms with 15 children, teacher aides, and apparently lots of money. These were nothing like our classrooms. You could feel the tension in the air.

When I left the meeting, I almost felt that we should scrap our transportation unit. So little progress had been made. It seemed so far away and much too difficult under the current circumstances. As I thought about it, I realized that maybe I had expected too much.

Kristine's story could have been quite different if she and her colleagues had incorporated four essential ingredients for successful theme building: an empowerment as curriculum writers, an awareness of all the options, a clear vision of the end product, and a workable model for theme building.

Empowerment as Curriculum Writers

Kristine, her colleagues, and those planning the district-wide meetings Kristine referred to, all seem to understand intuitively that the challenge of writing integrated thematic curriculum could best be met by teachers working collaboratively. However, when Kristine worked with teachers from different schools at the district-wide meetings, she left feeling confused and dissatisfied. These meetings did not provide enough time for the small groups of teachers from different schools to become true teams, with members trusting each other enough to express honest opinions and forge shared visions. Meanwhile, at her own school, Kristine was already part of a helpful team. Her team of second grade teachers had built a relationship of mutual support and trust. Furthermore, they shared planning time on a regular basis. These teachers knew well the needs of the students in their school. Kristine and her colleagues needed a clear charge from administrators that their school-based team was to build thematic curriculum together.

These teachers also needed to be given authority to make curriculum decisions. We can see throughout her journal that Kristine and her colleagues spent a lot of time and effort trying to figure out what someone else wanted from them. We're not sure who this someone was, perhaps a school administrator or curriculum consultant hired by the school system. Nevertheless, Kristine and her colleagues needed to focus instead on what they wanted—on what curriculum they would like to create to best meet the needs of their students. They needed to become a self-directed team.

The notion of empowerment through school-based teams is consistent with an educational reform movement gaining strength in America: school-based or site-based management. School-based management involves a decentralized shift of authority with control moving from states and districts to individual schools. The ultimate goal of this trend toward site-based decision making is improved student performance and improved school quality through the empowerment of school principals, teachers, parents, community members, and students. Traditionally, teachers have been left out of significant decision making and have been isolated from each other. Site-based management schools are offering teachers significant opportunities for involvement (Drake, 1993; McIntire & Fessenden, 1994; Mohrman & Wohlstetter et al., 1994).

Teachers are most enthusiastic about being involved in those decisions that impact their classrooms most directly, such as curriculum and instruction decisions (Johnston & Germinario, 1985). Therefore, in many districts using school-based management, teachers have an expanding role in curriculum design and decisions. Increasingly, central staff are serving as facilitators and resources in curricular matters.

These school-based activities are carried out by teams, empowered as decision makers. Even the most willing teachers find that working in isolation to create and deliver curriculum can be a difficult, if not overwhelming, task. Moreover, many districts believe that curriculum decisions should not rest with individual teachers. They maintain that the best curriculum decisions result from thoughtful discussion and collaboration. Teams of teachers and staff from the same school collaborate on curriculum activities such as theme building using the known interests, needs, and abilities of the student population as well as the expectations of the parents and community. Teachers find collaborative theme building to be supportive, encouraging, and stimulating. Any change is challenging, and curricular change is no exception. Working through ambivalence, uncertainty, and inevitable frustrations is a much more productive process when approached collaboratively. School-based curriculum teams can also achieve a balance of themes throughout the entire school, something that is not possible when each individual teacher is developing her own themes.

One of the greatest challenges for school-based management in general, and curriculum design in particular, is time (Ceperley, 1991).

Teachers writing theme studies collaboratively need administrative support in the form of significant release time for curriculum development activities. Another major obstacle the research identifies is the lack of training and knowledge in group process skills and human relations skills (Mohrman & Wohlstetter et al., 1994). School-based management depends on the effectiveness of teams in solving problems and making decisions. Traditionally, only administrators have been trained in these processes. In school-based management teams, all participants need support with team development and human relations issues.

Thus, Kristine needs to be empowered to build theme studies, to be part of a school-based curriculum writing team that is self-directed, to be trained in team building skills, and to be supported with the time and money needed to develop curriculum. In part, this book is designed to assist groups of teachers with the knowledge and skills required for developing into effective self-directed teams.

Awareness of Options

If teachers are to become self-directed builders of integrated, thematic curriculum, they need to know the full range of options available to them. Teachers building theme studies will find a wide variety of theme focus possibilities, multiple ways to identify theme boundaries, many alternative formats to describe the curriculum, and several effective paths within a structured model for accomplishing the curriculum building process. Teachers should consider the numerous options for team organization, team composition, role assignments, and mechanics. Additionally, as teachers implement theme studies in their classrooms, they will have options related to how much of the curriculum is integrated, ways of empowering students, types of instructional strategies to use, and ways of assessing learning. Once they know the options, theme builders can make the best choices for their particular circumstances. Empowered teachers assume responsibility for sorting through the options rather than trying to succeed with the same option that is working for teachers at a different school, whose situation might be quite different. Unlike many books on thematic curriculum that advocate one type of theme focus, one way to teach themes, or one carefully defined curricular product, this book sets forth the options so that teams can decide what is best for their schools.

A Vision of the End Product

Before a curriculum writing team can do its work, it needs a clear vision of the end product. There are two possible products for final integrated thematic curriculum plans: a teaching unit plan or a resource unit plan. A teaching unit includes a set of related lessons and activities selected to develop the most important understandings of a theme. Generally, a teaching unit also provides the overall unit objectives, a summary or outline of the major content and topics, a description of the daily flow or sequencing of lessons, and a description of the exact assessments to be used.

Unlike a teaching unit, a resource unit serves as a guide to multiple resources and ideas that can be selected and adapted to specific classes. It typically offers many optional activities and lessons, a summary of the major content, an extensive list of resources, alternative ideas for assessments, and a set of global concepts or essential understandings defining the range of the theme study.

We agree with Lounsbury (1992) that resource units are the more appropriate product for curriculum writing teams to envision and create.

> Teachers in common planning time or sometimes in summer workshops develop a unit fully, selecting activities each can use to achieve the objectives agreed on which relate to a particular subject's curriculum. The result is that all too often an interdisciplinary unit only teaches better what probably shouldn't be taught in the first place and leaves students as the passive consumers of others' decisions, much as they were in departmentalized instruction. The planning done by teachers apart from students should be to develop a *resource unit* not a *teaching unit*. Drawing on various options and an abundance of ideas in a resource unit, the teacher and students together should fashion the actual teaching unit. (Lounsbury, 1992, p. 157)

A THEME BOX AS A CURRICULUM RESOURCE   Significant advance curriculum planning by a team of teachers can go a long way toward assuring that a theme study's maximum potential is achieved. This advance planning should result in a usable product for all the teachers in the school who might someday implement the theme. In our view, the most flexible and usable product of a curriculum team is the "Theme Box," which can be circulated through the school media center and made available to all teachers in the building. This Theme Box expands on a resource unit since a team-generated resource unit is the heart of the Theme Box. In the resource unit, the team publishes general understandings or concepts, guiding questions, content summaries, and performance assessments, all of which define the theme study boundaries. Teams may also decide to include information reports, graphic organizers, ideas for learning experiences across several disciplines, a glossary, a bibliography, and a resource list including human resources in the area. Unlike a teaching unit, this resource unit refrains from indicating all the specific learning outcomes or a specific set of required activities or experiences. Instead those decisions are up to each individual teacher implementing the theme study.

In addition to the resource guide, the Theme Box should also include selected pieces of literature, purchased teacher resources, and teacher-made materials. As individual teachers use the Theme Box, they are encouraged to make additions to the box, including samples of student work and annotations to the resource unit. Thus with a Theme Box, integrated thematic curriculum becomes a living curriculum, continually adapted and enhanced by those teachers and classes implementing it. Figure 1.2 gives an overview of the many different types of resources that a Theme Box can hold.

Once a team is empowered to write curriculum for its school, is informed about options, and is focused on a clear vision of its product, it is ready to profit from a structured but flexible process for theme building.

A Workable Model for Theme Building

A teacher can be a theme builder through both his curriculum designing role on a school-based team and his theme implementing role as a classroom teacher. Ideally, most curriculum team members will also implement the theme studies they have designed. However, in the model for theme building set forth in this book, a classroom teacher certainly might implement theme studies designed by teams other than his own. The teacher as theme builder is summarized in Figure 1.3.

In this model the functions, decisions, and activities of a school-based curriculum team are distinguished from those of teachers implementing the theme study. Likewise, the curricular product of the school-based team is distinct from the product of the implementing teachers. The mission of the school-based curriculum team is creating the Theme Box. Using the resources provided in the Theme Box, the implementing teachers create with their students the actual teaching units.

The integrated curriculum resulting from these theme building activities incorporates the decisions of the curriculum teams, the implementing teachers, and the students. This negotiation of a curriculum has several advantages. First, sharing responsibility results in greater confidence in all the decisions made and a school-wide sense of accountability, commitment, and support for excellence. Second, all shareholders are learning and refining important transferable skills and dispositions. Chief among these is the ability to work together as time, effort, and training are invested in acquiring interpersonal skills. Third, shared curriculum building is motivating. Everyone involved feels empowered and supported. Teaching becomes less lonely for teachers while learning becomes less passive for students. The last and primary

Figure 1.2   *Theme Box Content Suggestions*

Basic

Theme Resource Book

Theme-Related Literature

Supplemental Options (Purchased and/or Teacher-Made)

Purchased Theme Units

Literature-Related Resources: kits or individual pieces including activity books, teacher guides, manipulatives, pictures

Music: CDs, cassettes, videos, songbooks, instruments

Computer Software: programs, games, PowerPoint presentations, clip art collections, related web site lists, directed Internet searches

Presentation Aids: transparencies, graphic organizers, charts, posters, maps, models

Bulletin Board Materials: plans, bulletin board pieces, borders

Theme-Related Collections: poetry, riddles, jokes, story starters, pictures, recipes, postcards, stamps, bookmarks

Manipulatives: puppets, flannel graph pieces, paper dolls, cutouts

Models: dolls, cars, animals, planets

Games: card, board, file folder, matching, twister, memory

Puzzles: picture, crossword, word searches, scavenger hunts

Cards: biography, flash, fact, culture, picture

Costumes and Dress Up: clothes, hats, shoes, masks, props

Arts and Crafts: rubber stamps, lacing cards, painting sponges

Room Decorations: pictures, mobiles, signs, art reproductions, dioramas, posters

Artifacts: nests, seeds, thermometers, insect collections, stuffed birds, tools, instruments, barometers, magnets, chop sticks, sea shells

Kits: discovery, pretend, craft, dress up, chemistry

Background Information Materials: sample lesson plans, magazine articles, bibliographies

Sample Student Work: journals, stories, pictures, videos, projects

Figure 1.3 *A Model of the Teacher as Theme Builder*

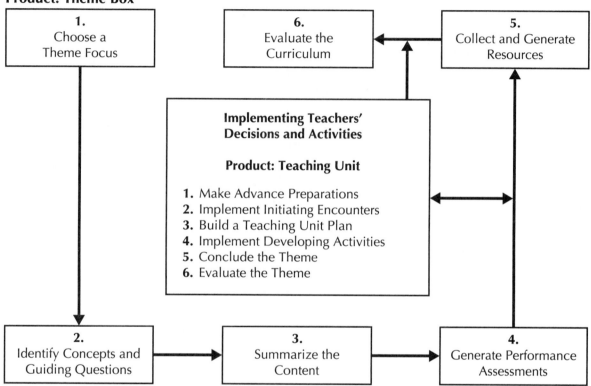

benefit of a curriculum negotiated by highly motivated, highly involved curriculum teams, implementing teachers, and students is a high quality usable product.

ROLES IN BUILDING AN INTEGRATED CURRICULUM Three shareholder groups—the curriculum team, the implementing teachers, and the students—have unique roles to play in negotiating the curriculum. If each group fulfills its responsibilities, it can fulfill the goals of building innovative curriculum, implementing exciting teaching units, and equipping lifelong learners.

The School-Wide Curriculum Teams' Role. A primary responsibility of school-wide curriculum teams is to maintain a broader perspective than would be possible for each individual teacher. Curriculum teams should have access to state requirements as well as district guidelines and initiatives. They should understand the full range of theme studies undertaken in the past and currently being planned in the school. By maintaining an overview of all this information, the curriculum teams can ensure that state, district, and student needs are balanced. For these reasons, the teams have the responsibility to determine the major themes to be studied in the school. In most cases, we advise teams to choose themes broad enough to give a great deal of flexibility to implementing teachers and students.

Once a team has chosen a theme focus, it must clearly establish the boundaries or parameters that will guarantee a coherent, purposeful, and substantial theme: concepts, guiding questions, content summaries, and performance assessments. Curriculum writing teams identify concepts and guiding questions by searching for the most universal, worthwhile, and transferable aspects of the theme. When these essential understandings are written as statements, they are called concept statements. When written as broad questions to guide learners, they are called guiding questions. Both concept statements and guiding questions are needed to establish the boundaries of a theme study. To further focus a theme study on what is valuable knowledge, the team prepares a summary of the content. Teams summarize content through information reports, content webs, or lists of content questions.

The next task of the school-based writing team is to design some alternative performance assessments that address the chosen concepts and guiding questions. Many assessment types are used throughout a theme study and most are designed by implementing teachers. However, because performance assessments are complex enough to encompass many, if not all, of the chosen concepts and guiding questions, they are best designed by the curriculum writing team. Teams of teachers can use their collective judgment and creative synergy to develop this kind of assessment.

Depending on the time available and the goal of the curriculum team, the team may generate and collect a variety of supplemental resources. In other instances, generating and collecting resources may be the responsibility of the implementing teachers. More often, though, this responsibility is shared between the curriculum team and the implementing teachers. Resources added to the Theme Box include activity ideas, teaching materials, and theme-related literature.

The final responsibility of the school-based team is to evaluate the curriculum. Evaluation of the parameters of the theme study as well as supplemental resources can be done only after field-testing the theme with implementing teachers and students. This evaluation should include significant input from the implementing teacher.

The Implementing Teachers' Role. Individual classroom teachers or teams of implementing teachers using the resources provided in a

Theme Box create specific teaching unit plans for specific students. The teaching plans accommodate some or all team-generated concepts but include additional objectives the teachers identified as important to their groups. These teaching plans are developed after two things have occurred: first, significant advance preparation using the Theme Box resources, and second, initial assessments and consultation with the students. The plans reflect student input as well as teacher judgment. Once constructed by teachers and students, the teaching units are implemented, concluded, and evaluated.

The Students' Role. In this model, students are expected to generate and share ideas, pose questions, and express preferences. They can expect support from their teachers but will come to realize that they are accountable for reaching certain decisions in collaboration with their classmates. Furthermore, students will have many individual choices to make. Their suggestions will be taken seriously and many student ideas will be incorporated into the negotiated curriculum. Figure 1.4 presents graphically the shareholders in an integrated curriculum.

Theme building and team building require work, commitment, and reflectivity, but the results are transferable to many educational efforts that teachers or students may pursue in the future.

Figure 1.4   *Shareholders in Building Integrated Curriculum*

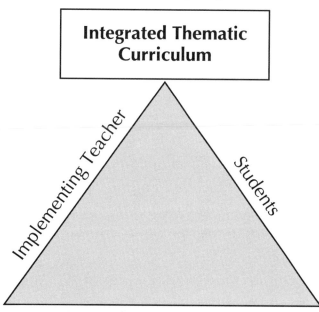

CONCLUSION

Teachers are looking for a way to mediate the demands on them to teach more content while motivating students to be engaged, lifelong learners. Integrated thematic curriculum is one promising approach. However, this curricular approach has demands of its own. Teachers are cast in the role of curriculum developer as well as curriculum implementer. But they can succeed in both those roles if they are empowered to make decisions. Teachers who work in the same school, have common planning time, and are self-directed have the potential to become empowered decision makers. Theme builders also need a full knowledge of their options, a clear vision of the end product, and a workable process for curriculum development. A flexible and usable product designed by a curriculum writing team to best serve the needs of the school-based curriculum effort is the Theme Box.

In Chapter 2, you are invited to explore the integrated thematic curriculum option more fully as you consider commonalties of all theme studies, significant differences among theme studies, advantages of theme studies for both teachers and students, and special challenges inherent in theme studies.

CHAPTER 2

Exploring the Nature of Integrated Thematic Curriculum

GUIDING QUESTIONS:

What Are the Critical Differences among Theme Studies?
What Are the Critical Elements All Theme Studies Share?
What Are the Advantages of Integrated Thematic Curriculum?
What Are the Special Challenges Inherent in Thematic Curriculum?

Integrated thematic teaching is an exciting model of teaching for teachers wanting to engage students in actively building their own understanding of important concepts. To judge its worth, however, teachers must understand the critical elements all effective theme studies share as well as the critical differences among theme study types that are caused by differing organizing focal points. To determine your willingness to commit to thematic curriculum development and teaching, you must carefully weigh the advantages and special challenges of this model, both for your students and for yourself.

To understand fully the nature of integrated thematic curriculum, consider again the question: What is a theme study? Most educators would agree that interdisciplinary thematic curriculum integrates ways of learning and content from more than one discipline and has a central focus. Curriculum writing teams must identify broad understandings related to the central focus for students to construct. By constructing lasting knowledge, students should find their world more understandable. The value of a theme study is enabling learners to move beyond the accumulation of fragmented information and facts to the pursuit of deep understanding of global concepts. Simultaneously, students are learning processes, strategies, and skills that can be transferred to future problem solving. Thus, a theme study can be defined as a relevant, in-depth study that makes interdisciplinary links, has a clear central focus, and leads to the construction of transferable knowledge and processes.

WHAT ARE THE CRITICAL DIFFERENCES AMONG THEME STUDIES?

While sharing a common definition, theme studies vary in nature primarily because educators have varying preferences for the central focus of a theme study. At least six major options prevail for the central or focal point of a theme study. These six focus types, along with examples of each, are detailed below.

1. A literature theme uses a single piece of literature or a related set of literature as the heart of the theme, such as *Number the Stars*, by Lowry (1990), or *Lyddie*, by Paterson (1991).
2. A topic theme starts with a general topic as a central focus and often addresses content in the science, social studies, or health areas. Many published theme studies fall into this category, using topics such as "Butterflies," "The Ocean," or "King Arthur's Court."
3. An abstract concept theme explores an idea, such as "interdependence," "change," or "patterns." This type of focus can also be combined with a topic, as in "interdependence in the community," "the changing horizon of exploration," and "patterns of immigration."
4. An event theme centers around a past, current, or future event or holiday. "The Summer Olympics," "Presidential Election 2000," or "Veteran's Day" fall into this category.
5. A problem theme begins with a real-life, open-ended problem or issue. Examples include an environmental issue such as "How can we clean up our air?" or a health concern such as "How does smoking affect our health and our quality of life?"
6. A position theme employs statements that take a position as the focal point. Examples include "Scientists should be limited in their research by standards of ethics" or "Everyone is responsible for keeping our town beautiful."

Should students study literature, topics, abstract concepts, events, open-ended problems, or position statements? Some educators strongly believe that one option is superior to the others; however, they do not agree on which option. We are convinced that all of these alternatives are appropriate as long as the theme study is worthy and substantial.

Above all, the theme must be designed to engage students in relevant and intellectually challenging study. Most teachers and preservice teachers we have worked with found it easiest to begin writing interdisciplinary thematic curriculum around topics, events, or literature. This is an excellent way to begin thematic planning. With experience, many teachers will find planning curriculum around abstract concepts, open-ended problems, or chosen positions an exciting alternative.

WHAT ARE THE CRITICAL ELEMENTS ALL THEME STUDIES SHARE?

While there are different types of themes and different ways to plan and implement them, certain characteristics are prominent in all worthwhile, meaningful theme studies. An examination of five critical elements will further understanding of the nature of theme studies: in-depth understanding, relevance, active inquiry, collaboration, and choices.

In-depth Understanding

Achieving complex, in-depth understanding is the first critical element of theme studies. Shallow coverage of many topics is replaced by more in-depth investigation of fewer topics. This search for deeper understanding will inevitably lead learners into interdisciplinary studies. The complexity of knowledge and continuity of ideas can only be embraced when teachers and students can freely cross artificial subject matter boundaries. In-depth understanding can best be achieved when students view important concepts and problems from many perspectives and disciplines. For example, students studying the problem of water pollution would need to examine economic, historical, political, geographic, and biological perspectives. Teachers need to consciously seek connections among various disciplines and fully use students' multiple ways of learning during the theme study to lead students to in-depth understanding.

Relevance

A second critical element in theme studies is relevance. Multidimensional learning that is connected to the students' real world is most likely to be seen as relevant. When learning is fragmented and piecemeal, students often lose sight of the relevance of their school work. Learners thrive on studying topics that are important and matter to them. Relevance is determined in part by what is engaging for students.

Certainly, enjoying learning is an important motivator for students, regardless of the focus of the studies or investigations. However, time in school is short. As good stewards of this time, responsible educators guarantee that themes also focus on educationally worthwhile content. In complex theme studies, relevance might be obvious to teachers but not to learners. In these cases, teachers need to help students see the connection between their studies and their lives. The best theme studies build explicitly on students' prior knowledge and background experiences. Theme study is an ideal teaching model for investigating worthwhile content that is important to students.

Active Inquiry

One defining attribute of thematic curriculum is heavy reliance on open-ended investigation. Unlike discovery learning, open-ended inquiry is investigation and research without a predetermined result. When the student is a problem solver, investigator, and researcher, the teacher becomes a facilitator. In most theme studies, some information is presented directly. Teacher, guest, media, and book presentations are all part of content-rich theme studies. However, while information can be directly provided, deep understanding requires active investigation from the learner. As students learn better researching skills, more responsibility for "finding out" can be relinquished to them. Thus, thematic curriculum development becomes a shared responsibility, with learners becoming the primary investigators.

Collaboration

Collaboration is a hallmark of both designing and pursuing integrated theme studies. School-based curriculum teams collaborate to design the fundamental parameters of theme studies. Teachers implementing theme studies collaborate with their students in creating a teaching unit plan. Students collaborate with each other, becoming a community of learners as they investigate ideas that matter to them. All learn to use each other's strengths, knowledge, and help. Parents, media specialists, and subject experts join teachers as human resources for students. One significant challenge for all adults collaborating with students engaged in theme studies is refraining from providing too much information or the solutions to problems. Instead, students need support in their investigations through a helpful structure that teaches critical thinking. Through experience, facilitating teachers learn when to step in to clarify confusion and when to step back to allow continued investigation. This step-in point varies with individual learners.

Choices

Another critical element of integrated thematic curriculum is the opportunity for everyone involved to be a decision maker. Teachers working together on school-based curriculum teams can be empowered to make decisions about the central focal points and boundaries of themes to be developed. However, classroom teachers and their students need to control most other decisions about the theme study as they make use of the multiple resources developed by the team. When implementing teachers and students in a school are entrusted with important decisions, they inevitably gain a sense of ownership in the curriculum.

This broad-based approach to decision making requires that those in authority at every level avoid making premature or preemptive decisions. Administrators and school boards should reflect on what choices are better left with curriculum teams. Curriculum teams need to guard against overplanning or overprescribing theme studies and learn to leave many decisions to the implementing teachers. Implementing teachers need to judiciously determine what decisions their students can help to make.

For some educators, the concept of students as curriculum decision makers is new. However, students prove themselves competent to generate their own questions about a theme and make decisions about ways to answer those questions. In some circumstances, students might choose the areas of a theme that interest them most and become "experts" on those aspects. Students can be given choices from a set of optional activities or projects. Often students can help to decide the ways in which they will show what they have learned and thus have a role in assessment. Clearly, giving choices requires extending trust, setting high expectations, and supporting risk taking for all participants. However, the results are worth it: Everyone grows.

WHAT ARE THE ADVANTAGES OF INTEGRATED THEMATIC CURRICULUM?

Like any other model of instruction, thematic teaching has unique strengths as well as undeniable challenges. Although this model is ideally suited to accomplish many educational goals, building integrated thematic curriculum involves facing special challenges for meeting both student and teacher needs. Teachers and administrators must be convinced that the advantages are significant enough to warrant the commitment required. The advantages for both students and teachers are summarized in Figure 2.1.

Figure 2.1 *A Summary of the Advantages of an Integrated Curriculum for Students and Teachers*

Advantages for Students	Advantages for Teachers
Increased Motivation	Increased Motivation
Greater Amounts of Learning	Greater Flexibility
Deeper Understanding	
Lifelong Learning Strategies	
Interpersonal Strategies	
Autonomous Learning Strategies	

The Advantages for Students

Students benefit from integrated thematic curriculum in several important ways. First, as students experience the magic and excitement that comes from investigating interesting topics or problems, their motivation is increased. Second, students have access to many resources and can use them to follow obvious connections in learning, thus learning more. Third, students explore global concepts and make connections through cross-discipline study, thus reaching deeper understanding. Fourth, students follow an ideal model for developing lifelong learning skills, thus achieving self-direction. Fifth, students work in cooperative groups where they learn to collaborate with others. Thus, knowledge of interpersonal strategies is developed. Finally, students are involved in creating their own learning plans and classroom rules, thus growing as autonomous learners.

INCREASED MOTIVATION   Every teacher holds increased motivation, enjoyment, curiosity, and commitment to learning as important goals for students. The positive effects of integrated theme studies on motivation are well supported in educational research (Friend, 1984; Jacobs, 1989; Mansfield, 1989; Olarewaju, 1988; MacIver, 1990; Schell & Wicklein, 1993; and Wasserstein, 1995). Several features of thematic integrated curriculum promote higher motivation and enjoyment levels. One feature is that students working on larger projects with complex tasks more readily perceive the relevance of their learning. Instructional experiences are interconnected and more obviously purposeful. Learners also have more opportunities to pursue topics that interest them. They have more choices in what they learn and in the ways they demonstrate the understanding they have achieved. Integrated curriculum promotes student ownership by offering choices, shared control, and opportunities for self-regulation. Students engaged in theme studies learn that others value their ideas and contributions. Most integrated curriculum options promote some measure of risk taking, experimenting, and independent researching and thus encourage curiosity. Another possible explanation for the greater motivation experienced by students involved in integrated studies is the greater likelihood of having motivated, enthusiastic teachers. Because of increased student motivation, educators using this type of curriculum can expect increasingly positive dispositions toward school.

GREATER AMOUNTS OF LEARNING   Limited research is available regarding whether students engaged in integrated studies learn more of the traditional curriculum than students in a more traditional approach. Despite the limited research in this area, logic dictates that motivated students are inclined to learn more and remember information longer because of their intent to do so. Also, students master relevant and meaningful knowledge more easily and completely. Some theorists suggest that instruction that makes obvious connections between ideas is more in line with how the brain naturally processes information. Research by Cromwell (1989) and Caine and Caine (1991) found that the brain searches for patterns and connections. Integrated thematic curriculum builds on prior knowledge and experience and consciously attempts to strengthen connections.

Because integrated teaching typically surrounds the learner with more resources than the traditional curriculum, teachers can expect increased learning. More than workbooks, textbooks, and a classroom teacher is required if a theme is to be explored in depth. Typically, in theme studies, students have access to a wide range of human resources: a team of teachers, professional experts on the topic, classmates, media specialists, and parents. Technology resources as well as content resources are used throughout the study. This collaboration expands the community of learners beyond the classroom setting.

Additionally, in preschool and primary grades, thematic curriculum provides children with more opportunities to explore science, social studies, and health topics. In traditional early childhood classrooms where reading and math skills are the primary focus, these discipline areas receive limited exposure.

DEEPER UNDERSTANDING   Students study fewer topics in thematic curriculum, but they tend to arrive at a thorough, coherent understanding of significant global ideas and concepts. Less can be more: A study of fewer concepts and topics with many connections is preferable to covering many concepts and topics superficially. Time spent on in-depth investigations replaces time spent on surveying a wide variety of topics, practicing discrete skills (many already mastered), and accumulating soon-forgotten facts.

LIFELONG LEARNING STRATEGIES   Educators have come to value the cultivation of students' creativity, curiosity, reasoning abilities, and inquiry skills. Theme studies draw students deeper into content, thus provoking the use of process skills and strategies that enable learners to think more deeply and at higher levels of abstraction. With careful curriculum planning, theme studies are designed so students learn problem solving skills and analysis strategies as they answer perplexing questions.

To develop higher level thinking skills, teachers should build into their integrated theme studies an inquiry and active learning orientation. The emphasis on active learning is based in part on Piaget 's theory that physical activity is connected to mental stimulation and activity (Piaget, 1963). Students are encouraged to physically explore their environment, interacting with both people and objects. During this physical exploration, students participate in activities promoting thinking, problem solving, and decision making. Within this context, theme builders must make a conscious effort to provide experiences that encourage making decisions, weighing evidence, and using inventive thinking. Thus, as students construct understanding of the content that they are investigating, they are also developing lifelong autonomous learning skills, strategies, and dispositions. Process goals focusing on creativity, thinking skills, and problem solving are unified with goals focusing on mastery of content throughout the theme studies. Dispositions such as curiosity, responsibility, cooperation, and self-direction are cultivated.

INTERPERSONAL STRATEGIES   Integrated thematic teaching approaches rely a great deal on working with others. Cooperative learning is one model of group work often used in thematic teaching. At times, teachers may want to create heterogeneous groups by balancing such factors as academic ability, gender, cultural background, and race. Cooperative learning is an ideal teaching model for promoting goals of accepting diversity, appreciating others, and gaining more cooperative attitudes (Sharan, Kussell, Hertz-Lazarowitz, Bejarano, Raviv, & Sharan, 1984; Johnson, Rynders, Johnson, Schmidt, & Haider, 1979). Slavin (1986, 1995) has produced compelling evidence that the cooperative learning model increases academic learning as well as social skills. However, to guarantee optimal results in achievement and cooperation, teachers must hold positive and high expectations for all group members. Because all students benefit from trying out dominant team roles, high achieving students should be prevented from always assuming these roles. In addition, all students are likely to benefit most from cooperative learning when group members go beyond simply sharing information with each other. Cooperative learning groups should be environments where students explain ideas to each other, discuss readings, invent models, develop systems for organizing information, and solve problems.

AUTONOMOUS LEARNING STRATEGIES Theme studies also provide opportunities for self-directed learning and self-regulation. In order to maximize the potential for autonomous learning, teachers must take seriously students' hunches, hypotheses, opinions, interests, and decision making abilities. As students make plans, test their ideas, and make choices about their learning, they become more confident in their competence and grow as autonomous, independent learners. Because theme studies generally provide many ways to learn and many possibilities for investigating, students will become increasingly willing to take risks in posing questions and searching for answers. Students involved in creating classroom rules, guidelines for activities, and criteria for evaluating their work gain experience in self-regulation. Theme studies fulfill the goals of producing self-direction, self-knowledge, self-regulation, and self-esteem.

The Advantages for Teachers

Teachers using an interdisciplinary curriculum usually find this an exciting way to teach. They find it motivating to work with a curriculum that maximizes both their own creativity and that of their students. The possibilities of such a curriculum are endless, thus allowing teachers greater flexibility in how and what they teach.

INCREASED MOTIVATION One teacher who regularly builds theme studies with colleagues described herself to us as a "born again" teacher. She reported that her teaching has become energized since she began designing and teaching theme studies. Increase in motivation is commonly experienced by teachers successfully moving toward planning and implementing integrated thematic curriculum (Berlin and Hillen, 1994). Several factors might account for the satisfaction and excitement that teachers experience, not the least of which is the joy of seeing students excited about the magic of learning. Furthermore, integrated thematic curriculum allows as much room for the creativity of teachers as for the creativity of students. Endless possibilities for connections, inquiry, and reflection exist. Teachers, as well as students, continually will be learning new facts and skills, and gaining deeper understanding of important ideas. Teachers planning and implementing an integrated curriculum are less professionally isolated because they network with a community of teachers and students and collaborate with colleagues. Last, integrated thematic curriculum promotes a sense of ownership and pride in the curriculum because it is created by the teachers themselves, working together.

GREATER FLEXIBILITY Integrated thematic curriculum emphasizes building knowledge from many disciplines and many experiences. It also draws upon the multiple intelligences, skills, learning styles, and experiences of teachers and students. This openness to possibilities makes the curriculum flexible for teachers. Teachers are no longer tied to a lock-step progression through a sequence of skills or textbook topics. Teachers are freed from narrow lessons having one or two behaviorally prescribed objectives. Holistic, experiential activities having many possible goals are the norm. Teachers have flexibility in scheduling time, using resources, integrating topics, and grouping students.

WHAT ARE THE SPECIAL CHALLENGES INHERENT IN THEMATIC CURRICULUM?

Both students and teachers can benefit greatly from the advantages of an integrated, thematic curriculum. However, both students and teachers have needs that present special challenges for this type of curriculum. Knowledge of these needs and a plan to meet them can ensure that teachers successfully write and implement theme studies and that all students successfully construct knowledge and build new connections. Figure 2.2 summarizes the needs of students and teachers that present special challenges when writing integrated thematic curriculum.

Special Challenges for Meeting Student Needs

While students benefit significantly from integrated thematic studies, teachers may need other curriculum models to provide variety and fully meet student needs. In addition, if theme studies are going to fulfill their potential, they must offer unifying substance that will accommodate the needs of all types of learners.

Figure 2.2 *A Summary of Special Challenges to Curriculum Writers*

Student Needs	Teacher Needs
Variety	Planning Time
Substance	Structure
Individual Accommodation	Support

NEED FOR VARIETY   The many benefits of integrated thematic teaching might lead one to think educators have at last found "the only way to go." To the contrary, at times students need to be engaged in discipline-based studies in order to learn the unique structure, perspective, methods, and language of each discipline. Additionally, teachers are concerned that basic skills may not be addressed or practiced sufficiently in a theme study. While emphasis on mastering skills is the strength of the traditional curriculum, the modeling and practicing of strategies and skills is essential work in any classroom meeting the needs of elementary and middle school students. To a large extent, strategies and skills can be taught within natural, meaningful contexts as students investigate essential questions in their theme studies. Many skills can be effectively taught through minilessons when a skill is needed to complete a more meaningful task. For example, students can be taught ways to search for the main idea when they are researching a topic. They can be taught library skills when they have an authentic need to use library resources. However, current projects and themes may not present sufficient opportunities for the practice of some important skills. Teachers must have knowledge of the non-negotiable skills for which they are responsible. When the integrated curriculum does not present meaningful contexts for their development or sufficient opportunities for practice, teachers must augment the integrated curriculum with more focused skill work.

Just as incorporating all essential skills into theme studies is difficult, so is incorporating all the disciplines into any one particular theme. Unnatural alliances or forced connections are to be avoided. When necessary, teachers must use other models of instruction to make sure all disciplines receive sufficient time and attention. For example, when implementing a predominantly social studies theme topic, a teacher might initiate a project approach to engage the students in science investigations, or a more science-oriented theme might be scheduled next. If math is not easily or sufficiently connected to the theme, the teacher might choose a math workshop approach for a period of time.

NEED FOR SUBSTANCE   An equally serious challenge is meeting the student need for themes of substance. The danger is that some theme topics may be treated superficially with an emphasis on appeal rather than potential for deep understanding. For example, in some published theme studies topics are treated in much the same way as the theme parties we plan for young children. Planning and throwing a birthday party with the theme of dinosaurs or rain forests is fun for everyone, but it would be hard to prove that anything significant is learned about dinosaurs or rain forests at such events. Buzzing with possible art ideas or delightful literature options for a theme on butterflies, teachers may fail to give thought to the lasting knowledge that might be gained by an in-depth study and observation of actual butterflies. Too many interdisciplinary units become a sampling of activities from several disciplines without revealing much unifying substance. Themes where the focus, important concepts, guiding questions, and essential content are given serious thought have the potential to become themes of substance and cohesiveness.

NEED FOR INDIVIDUAL ACCOMMODATION   Another possible challenge is that the typical theme study approach may not appeal to some learners or may not address their learning style differences. Predominantly linear thinkers might need more structure than is provided. In addition, students who are reluctant to assume initiative and those who do not enjoy group work may dislike the collaborative nature of many integrated themes. Teachers who are sensitive to their students' individual needs can use the flexibility of theme work to provide adaptations. For example, a teacher might assist a student who needs structure in making a detailed action plan for his research project. Likewise, a teacher would want to place students needing more support in appropriate heterogeneous groups. Adjustments in expectations for the products and performances of individual learners are also necessary.

Special Challenges for Meeting Teacher Needs

As motivating as integrated thematic teaching is for teachers, it can also be frustrating unless they realistically address certain potential challenges. Teachers need to be given significant amounts of planning time to develop curriculum for a theme study. They also require a workable structure because of the complexity of the tasks of designing and effectively implementing interdisciplinary studies. Support from administrators, parents, and colleagues empower teachers to use this model successfully.

NEED FOR PLANNING TIME   Teachers quickly realize that the greatest challenge to an integrated curriculum is time. Our own studies reveal that the time required for a curriculum planning team to thoroughly research and develop a theme study is on the average 150 hours, with approximately 20 hours spent in team meetings and around 30 to 40 hours spent by each team member in independent work. Time data was gathered from teams of three or four inservice or preservice teachers developing their first Theme Boxes. Our calculations are surprisingly similar to those of Jacobs (1989) whose studies revealed an average of 164 hours including planning both before and during theme implementation. Teams in Ontario found that ten days was an optimal amount of time for collaboratively building a theme unit (Drake, 1993). The time commitments necessary are often a shock to teachers and administrators. However, as they gain experience in building theme studies, teachers can become more efficient with preparation time.

Since theme building is so open-ended, some groups always see ways to improve and expand and find it difficult to finish their work. Therefore, curriculum writing teams need to plan time commitments in advance and create the best possible product within that time frame. Administrators and teachers must face the reality that thematic curriculum development is time consuming if they want to reap the benefits of integration.

NEED FOR STRUCTURE Another challenge facing teachers is the seemingly endless possibilities of theme building. Not only is thematic curriculum writing time consuming, but it also can be overwhelming. A structure for planning and implementing curriculum must be instituted so that starting points, check points, and evaluation points can be established. Creating an efficient way to move through the process, such as the one provided in this book, greatly lessens the frustrations. However, every team must find its own way to work and adapt the recommendations of other educators.

NEED FOR SUPPORT A third challenge is obtaining support from both the administration and parents. Often a lack of support comes from a lack of knowledge. If administrators cannot envision ways that district and state objectives can be met through thematic teaching, they may hesitate to support curriculum teams and implementing teachers. For some parents, this approach to learning may seem like too much fun and vastly different from the way they were taught. Parents may also be concerned that their children are not learning some of the basic skills in the way that they learned, through drill and repetition. When dealing with both parents and administrators, communication is the key. As a curriculum writing team shares goals, objectives, and then results, its support base will grow.

Teachers writing and teaching integrated curriculum need a base of support because they are continually facing the challenge of change. Even when exciting and energizing, change can be stressful. The changes brought by integrated, thematic instruction are significant, not only in the way teachers plan instruction but in the ways they teach as well. New instructional strategies and management strategies must be integrated into existing ones and in some cases must replace outdated ones.

Why would teachers want to throw themselves into work requiring so much stretching in so many new directions? We have observed over and over again that despite the inevitable uncertainties that change brings, teachers get caught up in the joy of learning and creating as they build themes. The satisfaction, pride, and ownership they feel in the curriculum they have developed result in most of them advocating that all teachers try some thematic planning and teaching. A student in our teacher education program had this to say after completing her first Theme Box with a team: "I am shocked that I learned to create integrated thematic curriculum in so short a time. Even the word curriculum seemed so overwhelming at first. The product our team created is something I am very proud of. I have come to realize that working with others and committing myself to excellence aren't easy, but the results are fantastic. Every teacher should try this." When all aspects are weighed, the balance is not in doubt; meeting the challenges of integrated thematic teaching is worth the effort.

CONCLUSION

Interdisciplinary thematic teaching is a unique model of teaching with its own critical elements, focus options, advantages, and special challenges. Differences among theme studies result primarily from differences in the central focus. The six major types of theme studies are literature, topic, abstract concept, event, problem, and position. Regardless of the theme study type, all themes of excellence share five critical elements: in-depth understanding, relevance, active inquiry, collaboration, and choices. Both teachers and students enjoy several advantages in integrated thematic curriculum. However, when employing this type of curriculum, teachers also will have special challenges in meeting student needs as well as their own needs.

Thematic curriculum development is done best by groups of teachers who are self-directed and work to become unified effective teams. Chapter 3 describes ways for curriculum writing teams to become supportive, productive teams.

CHAPTER 3

Exploring Team Building

GUIDING QUESTION:

What Is an Effective Team?

We believe that the best way to create curriculum is through school-based curriculum teams. The model presented in this book is a negotiated curriculum, whose principal shareholders are school-based curriculum writing teams, implementing teachers, and student groups. To work effectively on teams, both as curriculum writers and implementers, teachers should take time to understand what teams are and how they work.

WHAT IS AN EFFECTIVE TEAM?

In the past, traditional work groups were referred to as teams. However, members of traditional work groups took directions from a leader or boss, had preset goals, and often sought personal rewards, leading to competition among teammates. When problems arose, the focus was on who or what to blame. Working on these "teams" could be challenging and nonproductive.

> Traditional organizational structures really do not demand much in the way of individual contributions from their participants. What is demanded is an adherence to the hierarchical chain of command and a willingness to carry out instructions and obey orders. . . . Training requirements are minimal because once a worker has been told what his or her job requires, little else is expected of that employee.

In a high-involvement organization, however, employees are expected to think, contribute, and work together. . . . To be successful, employees need to know how to interact, how to work together to solve problems, how to reach a consensus in groups, how to communicate, how to collaborate, and how to evaluate ideas and suggestions. Training to develop these skills needs to be extensive and broad based. (McIntire & Fessenden, 1994, p. 102)

To a large extent, today's curriculum writing team should be a self-directed team. This means taking initiative, working with available resources, finding creative ways to improve the quality of its school's curriculum, concentrating on preventing crises, and working together to solve problems. Team members cooperate and focus on team contributions and achievements, continually improving and innovating to create the best products. Working on a self-directed team is usually energizing and rewarding.

A curriculum writing team should be composed of educators who define and work toward a common goal. Building on each other's strengths and ideas, members produce an innovative, exciting, and usable product. Team members must realize that they are doing two things simultaneously: developing into an effective self-directed working team and writing curriculum. Both activities require deliberate discussion and effort. For this reason, jumping into the task of curriculum development with little knowledge of teams and their development can be detrimental to team building. In some situations, formal training in interpersonal skills or exercises in building trust may be necessary. In every situation, there needs to be time spent at the beginning and throughout the theme building process in learning how teams work and communicate. Researchers and experienced team builders invariably consider training the most important influence on the success of self-directed schools (McIntire & Fessenden, 1994; Mohrman & Wohlstetter et al., 1994). Before exploring teams further in this chapter, use Action Pack 3-1 to record the advantages and disadvantages of teamwork you have experienced in the past. (A note about Action Packs: Action Pack pages guide teams through the tasks involved in writing integrated thematic studies. Your team can use Action Pack pages in the ways that best meet your needs.)

Advantages of Working in Teams

Why do we promote working in school-based teams for curriculum writing? Earlier, we mentioned one disadvantage of integrated thematic curriculum development: the amount of time required. A team allows you to divide the time, labor, and effort needed to produce excellent thematic curriculum. The old adage, "many hands make light work," is true; not only is the work load divided but the act of collaborating is rewarding. Teaching can be a lonely profession, allowing little time to interact with peers. The chance to work with other teachers on teams provides sharing, encouragement, and support. Not only do teachers support each other during integrated curriculum development, but they discover that the team brings increased support for the final product. Teachers collaborating on curriculum will be more motivated and accountable to implement that curriculum. They also will be more inclined to encourage other teachers to implement integrated theme units. Furthermore, collaborating with others brings an increased knowledge and skill base to your project from the very beginning. Every subject matter expert (SME) on your school-based team lessens the amount of outside help needed or additional research that the team must undertake.

An additional advantage for preservice teachers who work on thematic curriculum development teams is the opportunity to practice teamwork skills they will need on a "real" job. Today's teachers work on grade level teams, subject matter teams, governance groups, and action research committees throughout the school year. In addition to cultivating practical skills in working with others, understanding how one's teaching potential is enhanced through collaboration with other professionals is always valuable. For inservice teachers, working on a team to develop a Theme Box will provide a chance to practice some of the same skills their students will need in cooperative learning activities. Experiencing the same kinds of joys and difficulties as student groups can make teachers more sensitive to students' feelings and fears. Experience in teamwork aids teachers in anticipating and avoiding problems when students work in teams.

However, the greatest benefit of teamwork for teachers is the creative energy flow or synergy generated by collaboration. This contagious excitement motivates the team to build on one another's ideas, talents, skills, energies, and efforts. Synergy accomplishes what no one person can do individually: it dramatically adds to the individual development and accomplishments of each team member. "We are greater than the sum of our parts" is another adage that has been proven time and time again in our observation of curriculum writing teams. Figure 3.1 summarizes these advantages.

Building a Winning Team

In their careers, most teachers have already had extensive experience with working in groups. However, many of these groups could not be considered teams. A team is a joint effort that should start with choosing members thoughtfully and end with a unified, productive group and

Figure 3.1   *Summary of the Advantages of Teamwork*

> 1. Decreases time requirements.
> 2. Divides labor requirements.
> 3. Increases the knowledge base.
> 4. Builds transferable teamwork skills.
> 5. Promotes collegiality, sharing, and mutual support.
> 6. Builds widespread commitment for the product.
> 7. Produces a better product.
> 8. Generates creative synergy.

an innovative high quality product. Choosing team members is an important first step. The best teams are composed of willing volunteers. Beyond this, it is important that team members have areas of diversity as well as areas of uniformity. Ideally, the team should be diversified in working styles, multiple intelligences, skills, and knowledge while unified in philosophy and commitment. Figure 3.2 identifies commonalties and diversities in effective teams.

PERSONAL WORKING STYLES   Knowing the personal working styles of prospective team members can help you choose a balanced and productive team. Even if your team has been prechosen or self-selected, knowledge of working styles can help you to effectively use each team member's strengths and talents. One of the greatest assets of a team is that its members are different in the ways that they work and in their points of view. Researchers apply different names for these personal work or preference styles but generally define them as "the set of preferred behavior patterns that we exercise most of the time, in most situations, and with most people" (McIntire & Fessenden, 1994, p. 65). The most effective teams come to terms with the reality of differing styles and turn this diversity to their advantage. Clearly, teamwork requires that team members understand and respect the fact that people have different perspectives and different approaches to accomplishing tasks. Team members need to expect these differences, discuss them, and seek creative ways to use them.

In groups we have worked with, we have witnessed inexperienced people who were eager to benefit from working with more experienced team members. We have also seen *linear thinkers,* who were originally frustrated by more *intuitive, creative thinkers,* who came to understand the benefits of these differences. Additionally, we have seen close friends open their circle to admit a new person with a different viewpoint. Overcoming initial hesitation, these groups succeeded not only in producing a curriculum Theme Box, but also in becoming a team.

Figure 3.2 *Characteristics of Effective Teams*

Commonalities	Diversities

Shared dispositions
  will take initiative
  will work with available resources
  will work to prevent problems
	Personal workstyles
	
	Interests
	
	Skills
	
	Knowledge
	
	Multiple intelligences profile

Shared vision and goals	

Shared values
  for interdisciplinary teaching
  for collaborative team building	

One step toward becoming an effective team is in getting to know and trust your teammates. Discussing preferred workstyles is one avenue to learning about teammates. Before reading further, use the workstyle characterizations on Action Packs 3-2 and 3-3 to identify your own workstyle and to facilitate team discussion. A brief profile of each workstyle follows.

The *People Person* is sensitive to individual members' needs. He focuses on the team's social goals as well as product goals, giving priority to team processes and team building. This group member is often a peacemaker who strongly values group unity. This supportive member helps others find and use unique strengths. A people person usually encourages others and mediates in consensus building and conflict resolution.

The *Idea Person* is creative, visionary, and willing to take risks. Many idea people can generate enthusiasm for innovation. The idea person is likely to put forth new theories and approaches for the group's consideration—even when a group thinks a final decision has been reached. She is usually ready to take on challenges and learns by jumping into a project. Persuasive and assertive, she often influences others' decision making. An idea person is characteristically comfortable with ambiguity.

The *Detail Person* is task oriented, analytical, and typically cautious until he can see how all the pieces will fit. For him, an important goal is addressing details accurately. His low tolerance for fuzzy thinking helps the team achieve clarity. The detail person is often focused, organized, punctual, and skilled in research. This person enjoys solving problems by examining multiple options but may be dissatisfied with less-than-perfect solutions.

The *Take Charge Person* is goal oriented and focused on organizing the practical aspects that will result in getting the job done. The take charge person skillfully manages time, resources, and agendas. He often forces decisions that will move the group ahead. He helps the team stay on task and meet deadlines. His approach to problem solving is rational, objective, and logical. A take charge person's major goal is getting the product completed on schedule.

Although everyone has traits from more than one style, one workstyle will almost always predominate. Figure 3.3 shows some strengths and weaknesses of each workstyle. Awareness of one anothers' workstyles helps the team to anticipate possible problems and prevent conflict.

> LINDA: *I was introduced to the value of considering workstyles when I was an assistant manager of a large corporation. A new manager took over my unit and we continually ran into problems in our approaches to the job. Because I had been in my position for many years and am an "idea person," I often worked from instinct. My manager was a "detail person" who was demanding studies and statistics to back up my decisions. I felt that he lacked trust in my abilities, until I took a company course on workstyles. I immediately recognized our differing workstyles. With this new understanding, I was able to go back to my workplace and forge a better relationship with my manager. As I willingly volunteered more details and facts, he began to trust my abilities when I wanted to try something new and innovative.*

A little thought makes it apparent that a team of four "detail people" would be a team that could become bogged down in specifics without ever achieving a broad vision of its work or a manageable plan. On the other hand, a team of "idea people" could dream innovative visions lacking the specifics that would make their product most useful to others. A mix of identified strengths makes the most productive teams. Workstyle knowledge is especially important on preselected teams. Evaluating teammates' workstyles can point out places where each member's strengths can best be used. If the team is lacking strengths associated with a particular workstyle, it can plan ahead to compensate for any areas of team weakness. Some team members can comfortably adapt their workstyles to meet the group needs. Anticipating and preventing problems will ensure that any team can effectively meet its goals.

Sometimes a team member may view himself differently than others do or may behave differently when part of a team. Knowledge of these differences in perceptions can be important to team unity. After your team has worked together for a while, you can use Action Packs 3-4 and 3-5 to evaluate each other's workstyles. Compare this information to your view of your personal workstyle.

Figure 3.3 *Some Characteristics of Four Workstyles*

People Person

Strengths		Weaknesses	
dependable	encouraging	conforming	following
generous	helpful	emotional	indecisive
loyal	peacemaking	low risk taking	nondiscriminating
social	supportive	passive	possessive
sympathetic	team playing		

Idea Person

Strengths		Weaknesses	
charismatic	creative	dreaming	impulsive
dramatic	dreaming	oversimplifying	short on follow
enthusiastic	influential	tolerant of	through
innovative	motivating	ambiguity	undisciplined
multidimensional	optimistic	unrealistic	unreachable
			goal setting

Detail Person

Strengths		Weaknesses	
accurate	analytical	anxious	cautious
conscientious	detail oriented	close minded	impersonal
hard working	high standards	judgmental	overthinking
prompt	self-disciplined	perfectionistic	rigid
systematic	task oriented		

Take Charge Person

Strengths		Weaknesses	
decisive	direct	autocratic	competitive
energetic	fast thinking	controlling	impatient
forceful	organized	insensitive	intolerant
planning	product oriented	nonreflecting	stubborn
risk taking	self-confident		

MULTIPLE INTELLIGENCES   Knowing the multiple intelligences can also help you build a balanced team. In 1983, Howard Gardner introduced his theory of multiple intelligences in the book *Frames of Mind.* He rejected the idea that human beings have a single type of intelligence and instead theorized that they have several distinct, identifiable intelligences. According to his theory, everyone has all of the intelligences but with unique patterns of strengths. Gardner defines an intelligence as the ability to solve problems or to make something that is valued in one or more cultures. As of this printing, Gardner's eight intelligences are categorized as: verbal linguistic, logical mathematical, spatial, bodily kinesthetic, musical, interpersonal, intrapersonal, and naturalistic. Persons with strengths in one or more intelligences will be uniquely qualified to fill needed roles on your team. Knowing multiple intelligences is valuable not only in team building but in many areas of writing and implementing thematic curriculum. The descriptions below will help your team to identify profiles of intellligences, clarify capabilities, and recognize learning preferences.

Verbal linguistic intelligence refers to the ability to use both oral and written language. A person with strong verbal intelligence can use words to explain himself, build trust, and communicate ideas. Because he is a good listener, words help him understand others. He enjoys using language in both logical and artistic ways. For him, learning is best achieved through speaking, reading, writing, and listening.

Logical mathematical intelligence refers to the ability to see patterns in the world and in numbers and to think in abstractions. A person strong in this intelligence can work with cause-and-effect relationships; use numbers to conjecture, reason, and problem solve; follow rules; and find symmetry and patterns. She learns best by following a scientific step-by-step process while analyzing, categorizing, classifying, and problem solving.

Visual spatial intelligence refers to the ability to perceive the world accurately and to manipulate this perception internally. A person with strength in this intelligence can interpret graphs and maps; use color, form, and space to design both practical and artistic plans; and accurately read plans to build and create things. This person learns best through observing and creating.

Bodily kinesthetic intelligence refers to the ability to use the body or parts of the body to solve problems, take effective actions, or put on a production. A person with strength in this intelligence can effectively use body language, construct things, perform athletically and/or artistically, and plan and critique the actions of his or others' bodies. This person learns best through movement in space, physical activities, role play, and touch.

Musical intelligence is the ability to sense pitch, tone, and patterns in music and respond to music. A musically intelligent person can remember and recreate the music around him, understand and use musical techniques, create and respond to expressive performances, and use music as a tool to meet others' needs. This person learns best through manipulating rhythm, melody, and rhyme.

Interpersonal intelligence refers to the ability to understand and notice differences in others. A person with strength in this intelligence can communicate well, work effectively in groups, organize and lead people, mediate and problem solve, and influence others. This person learns best through cooperative groups, team games, discussion, and relating to others.

Intrapersonal intelligence refers to the ability to know oneself and understand one's own strengths, weaknesses, and interests. A person with strength in this intelligence can work well independently, is centered and self-motivated, can follow instincts, and is capable of achieving goals. This person learns best through self-paced lessons, individual projects, journal writing and open-ended investigation.

Naturalistic intelligence refers to the ability to classify and recognize things in nature and to be sensitive to cycles in the natural world. A person with strength in this intelligence can interact with nature to provide for human needs, recognize and use patterns in nature for weather forecasting and other purposes, and find ways to balance the ecology. This person learns best through exploring and observing nature, discovering and relating to living things, and classifying and comparing aspects of the natural world.

On your team, choose members who provide strengths in as many of the eight intelligences as possible. Use Action Pack 3-6 to identify each team member's multiple intelligence profile. Once again, this knowledge is useful even if your team is prechosen, and will allow the team to use team members' strengths.

SKILLS AND KNOWLEDGE　Members should also be sought out for the unique skills and knowledge they can bring to the team. Who has expert knowledge in areas the team will be exploring? Who is an expert in the disciplines being integrated? Who has writing, editing, and researching skills? Who is especially creative? Who has highly developed computer knowledge and Internet skills? Who is recognized as especially knowledgeable about student interests and development? Who has the most current knowledge in instructional strategies? Who has worked effectively on teams in the past? Seek to find a balance of team members with contributions to make in these areas. Use Action Pack 3-7 to document members' interests, skills, and specialized knowledge.

When building a team, select members who provide diversity in work styles, multiple intelligences, skills, and knowledge. In these areas, diversity provides strength. If your team is prechosen, knowledge of members' differences will help the team to anticipate areas of weakness and plan ahead to compensate. On all teams, knowing and using team members' profiles of strengths can lead to building a winning team.

AREAS OF UNIFORMITY   While seeking a balance of diverse working styles, intelligences, skills, and knowledge, a team will find that uniformity is also important. The most important aspects are a commitment to the value of integrated thematic teaching and a willingness to work on team building. The best curriculum teams consist of members with positive dispositions and high expectations from team efforts. Teaching experience helps. Creativity helps. Good work habits help. But none of these is as important as philosophical compatibility and openness to working with colleagues. Ideally, a school-based curriculum writing team is a group of three to seven teachers whose common goal is the creating of one excellent theme study. Thus, within a school there might be several teams working simultaneously. There may well come a time when every teacher in a school is serving on a curriculum writing team. We recommend that the "pioneering teams" consist of volunteers with some theoretical understanding of and commitment to interdisciplinary teaching. A team of highly committed volunteers with a balance of experiences, skills, and knowledge is a team with a head start on the processes of theme development and team development. However, we recognize that in many situations, your team will be prechosen by an outside person such as a principal or curriculum consultant. Nevertheless, prechosen teams can become unified and productive if members are willing to commit to the teams and to integrated thematic curriculum.

Team Building Cycle

Every team goes through a cycle of trust building and team development. This is actually a cycle of change and challenge that can be applied to any collaborative endeavor, even curriculum writing. Drake (1993) called the stages of this cycle a journey.

On our journey with over 40 teams writing their first integrated theme studies, we have come to agree with Drake that while "these stages may seem to be presented as linear, they are most often experienced as chaotic and as 'two steps forward and one step back'" (1993, p. 7). In fact, our own journey diagram, shown in Figure 3.4, has been revised many times.

Figure 3.4   *Our Conceptualization of a Journey through the Team Building Cycle*

START UP AND CALL TO A CHALLENGE   If your team members are volunteers who value integrated curriculum and team work, they initially experience positive feelings: excitement, enthusiasm, and a sense of adventure. These positive feelings are likely to be mixed with some initial anxiety about roles and expectations. If team members are not volunteers, their initial anxiety may be even higher. Some team members may have had experience with previous team efforts that have left them cautious, if not resentful. Sharing stories of past experiences—both positive and negative—can be the beginning of trust building. The team can then resolve to work toward a better experience. A good device to begin that task is the worksheet presented in Action Pack 3-8. This Action Pack summarizes information that reveals areas of uniformity and diversity. Team members should complete this form individually and then share this information with the team. Sharing this information at the first team meeting is an effective way to begin getting to know one another.

REALITY CHECK   Once team members embark on the project itself, it is not unusual to be overwhelmed by the undertaking. Members soon realize that curriculum writing is complex work. Furthermore, the number of choices and possibilities can cause ambiguity, which makes some people uncomfortable. Tentative and anxious feelings are common. In addition, as team members gain knowledge of one another, differences in workstyles will become more apparent. It helps to remember that these feelings are to be expected in any new venture.

TRANSITION It takes time for a team to adjust to the changes required by the task and the need to accommodate different perspectives. Initially, everyone is polite and avoids any kind of conflict. Most team members are willing to share information and ideas at this point but may hesitate to share their feelings. All the while, each person is struggling inwardly with the need to accommodate different viewpoints, different personalities, and new ways of looking at curriculum. The team seems to function well at this point, but many issues are going unchallenged. There may be false consensus on some decisions.

FRUSTRATIONS AND STRUGGLES At first, individual adjustment to change, abandonment of old ideas, and adaptation to new team members is internal. When frustrations and uncertainty mount, members must share these issues with the team. In order for this to happen, trust must grow. Team members must be willing to share feelings, values, anxieties, and uncertainties. At this stage, conflicts may arise. Now people are struggling with change collectively rather than individually. This will be productive so long as members avoid certain pitfalls. One critical pitfall is excluding a member. When the viewpoints of one or two members are significantly different from those of the majority, members can be tempted to share frustrations with those who think as they do. Likewise, if one person seems less involved or committed, issues may be discussed without him. This should be avoided at all costs. The entire team needs to hear one another's opinions and take part in resolving the differences in expectations or viewpoints. Once a team successfully resolves a conflict or problem, its confidence grows. Trust in the team members and the group process grows as well.

ACCEPTANCE OF NEW PARAMETERS Eventually, each group member sees his role in creating a shared vision and is willing to leave behind his individual vision. Individual members come to terms with the need to change original notions as group goals are negotiated. Consensus seeking becomes the rule rather than the exception. Members look for ways to combine and strengthen ideas by using input from everyone in the group. The team is now ready to function as a unit.

BREAKTHROUGH At some point, a breakthrough occurs. Through consensus, the group reaches a common vision. At this point, the project progresses rapidly and smoothly. Once again, the group relives the excitement they experienced at the beginning, but it is enhanced by a new sense of confidence and direction.

UNITY AND PRODUCTIVITY   In groups where each member keeps his promises and fulfills his commitments, results are becoming visible and rewarding. Team members share leadership and provide valuable feedback to each other. This brings to the group a wonderful sense of accomplishment and power. Now a mutual trust level has been reached where the individual member is accountable to the team and the team is accountable to the individual member.

SHARED OWNERSHIP   Every team that reaches productive unity brings life to its creative visions and shares in a sense of ownership, pride, and joy. Members no longer compete for recognition, but share a sense of mutual accomplishment. One of the most exciting days for teams in our classes is an open house for family, friends, and other members of the education department. Theme Box contents are laid out in displays and visitors participate in sample learning activities. Professors, family members, and other students are always impressed with the quality of the curriculum writing. Teams share a sense of pride in their products and astonishment at what they have been able to accomplish together.

ADVOCACY   It takes a team many hours to write an integrated resource unit for a theme. Often the team has had moments of great uncertainty and discouragement. Sometimes the struggle for team unity has been painful. However, at the end of the process, theme building curriculum teams unfailingly recommend to others both theme building and team building. Moreover, team members are eager to be of service both to new collaborative writing teams and to implementing teachers. Some schools may want to take advantage of this desire to serve by having curriculum team members act as consultants to new curriculum teams who are starting their first Theme Boxes. This is the stage when team members can try their new skills in other settings. At this point, team members can help promote the team process and interdisciplinary curriculum development to others.

One way your team can evaluate the progress of your team development is to monitor your own journey. Action Pack 3-9 enables your team to discuss and evaluate your team's growth. Anticipating and understanding that cycles of change are inevitable and universal often help teams move through the rough spots and on to productivity more quickly.

Since a cycle of change is on-going, each time you work on a new team you will again go through stages similar to those in this cycle. However, knowledge and experience can make the progress more linear, with fewer setbacks. Even if your team completes one thematic study and decides to write a second, it will be undertaking the journey

again. This time, however, you will be moving toward unity and productivity more quickly as you build on your past teamwork experience.

CONCLUSION

Effective curriculum writing teams benefit from shared values, a shared
vision, and a shared work ethic. Beyond these commonalties, the best
teams are composed of members with diversified workstyles, intelligences, skills, interests, and areas of expertise. As each group of unique
members unites around the challenge of writing interdisciplinary curriculum, it can expect to go through a cycle of trust building and team
development. The cycle will involve some inevitable frustrations, anxiety, and adjustments before the team becomes united and productive.
    Chapter 4 explains several team mechanics that will enable a team
to achieve productivity by using its time and resources most effectively.

ADVANTAGES AND LIMITATIONS OF WORKING IN TEAMS

 **AP3-1**

Instructions: List the top five of the advantages and rewards as well as the limitations and frustrations that you have experienced working in teams.

Advantages and Rewards

1.

2.

3.

4.

5.

Limitations and Frustrations

1.

2.

3.

4.

5.

How could you design your team to maximize the advantages and minimize the disadvantages of working in teams?

1.

2.

3.

4.

5.

Instructions: In each list below, check the ten words that best describe you.

List One

accurate	analytical	charismatic
conscientious	creative	decisive
dependable	detail oriented	direct
dramatic	dreaming	encouraging
energetic	enthusiastic	fast thinking
forceful	generous	hard working
helpful	high standards	influential
innovative	loyal	motivating
multidimensional	optimistic	organized
peacemaking	planning	product oriented
prompt	risk taking	self-confident
self-disciplined	social	supportive
sympathetic	systematic	task oriented
team playing		

List Two

anxious	autocratic	cautious
close minded	competitive	conforming
controlling	dreaming	emotional
following	impatient	impersonal
impulsive	indecisive	insensitive
intolerant	judgmental	low risk taking
nondiscriminating	nonreflecting	oversimplifying
overthinking	passive	perfectionistic
possessive	rigid	short on follow through
stubborn	tolerant of ambiguity	undisciplined
unreachable goalsetting	unrealistic	

Now go to Action Pack 3-3 and highlight the characteristics you have checked under each workstyle. The area where you have highlighted the most characteristics is your predominant workstyle.

PERSONAL WORKSTYLE CHARACTERISTICS

 **AP3-3**

People Person

Strengths		Weaknesses	
dependable	encouraging	conforming	following
generous	helpful	emotional	indecisive
loyal	peacemaking	low risk taking	nondiscriminating
social	supportive	passive	possessive
sympathetic	team playing		

Idea Person

Strengths		Weaknesses	
charismatic	creative	dreaming	impulsive
dramatic	dreaming	oversimplifying	short on follow
enthusiastic	influential	tolerant of	through
innovative	motivating	ambiguity	undisciplined
multidimensional	optimistic	unrealistic	unreachable
			goalsetting

Detail Person

Strengths		Weaknesses	
accurate	analytical	anxious	cautious
conscientious	detail oriented	close minded	impersonal
hard working	high standards	judgmental	overthinking
prompt	self-disciplined	perfectionistic	rigid
systematic	task oriented		

Take Charge Person

Strengths		Weaknesses	
decisive	direct	autocratic	competitive
energetic	fast thinking	controlling	impatient
forceful	organized	insensitive	intolerant
planning	product oriented	nonreflecting	stubborn
risk taking	self-confident		

WORKSTYLE INVENTORY

 **AP3-4**

Instructions: In each list below, check the ten words that best describe your teammate.

List One

accurate	analytical	charismatic
conscientious	creative	decisive
dependable	detail oriented	direct
dramatic	dreaming	encouraging
energetic	enthusiastic	fast thinking
forceful	generous	hard working
helpful	high standards	influential
innovative	loyal	motivating
multidimensional	optimistic	organized
peacemaking	planning	product oriented
prompt	risk taking	self-confident
self-disciplined	social	supportive
sympathetic	systematic	task oriented
team playing		

List Two

anxious	autocratic	cautious
close minded	competitive	conforming
controlling	dreaming	emotional
following	impatient	impersonal
impulsive	indecisive	insensitive
intolerant	judgmental	low risk taking
nondiscriminating	nonreflecting	oversimplifying
overthinking	passive	perfectionistic
possessive	rigid	short on follow through
stubborn	tolerant of ambiguity	undisciplined
unreachable goalsetting	unrealistic	

Now go to Action Pack 3-5 and highlight the characteristics you have checked under each workstyle. The area where you have highlighted the most characteristics is your perception of your teammate's predominant workstyle.

People Person

Strengths		Weaknesses	
dependable	encouraging	conforming	following
generous	helpful	emotional	indecisive
loyal	peacemaking	low risk taking	nondiscriminating
social	supportive	passive	possessive
sympathetic	team playing		

Idea Person

Strengths		Weaknesses	
charismatic	creative	dreaming	impulsive
dramatic	dreaming	oversimplifying	short on follow
enthusiastic	influential	tolerant of	through
innovative	motivating	ambiguity	undisciplined
multidimensional	optimistic	unrealistic	unreachable
			goalsetting

Detail Person

Strengths		Weaknesses	
accurate	analytical	anxious	cautious
conscientious	detail oriented	close minded	impersonal
hard working	high standards	judgmental	overthinking
prompt	self-disciplined	perfectionistic	rigid
systematic	task oriented		

Take Charge Person

Strengths		Weaknesses	
decisive	direct	autocratic	competitive
energetic	fast thinking	controlling	impatient
forceful	organized	insensitive	intolerant
planning	product oriented	nonreflecting	stubborn
risk taking	self-confident		

Check the three or four intelligences that you perceive to be your greatest strengths.

____ **Verbal Linguistic Intelligence**

the ability to use and understand language; the ability to express yourself and to understand others through language.

____ **Logical Mathematical Intelligence**

reasoning ability; thinking in abstractions, ability to manipulate number operations; the ability to understand cause and effect.

____ **Visual Spatial Intelligence**

ability to visually depict information; the ability to represent the spatial world internally.

____ **Bodily Kinesthetic Intelligence**

ability to use whole body or parts of body to solve problems or put on productions.

____ **Musical Intelligence**

melody and rhythm abilities; ability to hear musical patterns.

____ **Interpersonal Intelligence**

ability to understand, empathize, and sympathize with others.

____ **Intrapersonal Intelligence**

ability to understand one's self and one's own needs.

____ **Naturalistic Intelligence**

ability to discriminate and classify living things; awareness of phenomena in the natural world.

Rate yourself either high (h), average (a), or low (l) on each of the following skills and areas of expertise.

_____ **1.** Computer literacy

_____ **2.** Internet skills

_____ **3.** Library research skills

_____ **4.** Writing skills

_____ **5.** Editing skills

_____ **6.** Organizational skills

_____ **7.** Listening skills

_____ **8.** Team building skills

_____ **9.** Time management

_____ **10.** Knowledge of child development

_____ **11.** Knowledge of instructional strategies

_____ **12.** Creativity

Personal Sharing Device

Name: _____

My educational background is:

My interests are:

Based on the personal workstyle characteristics (AP3-3), I would describe my personal workstyle as:

Based on Gardner's multiple intelligences (AP3-6), I would consider three of my strengths to be:

Based on the skill and knowledge checklist (AP3-7), the strengths I would bring to a team are:

Considering all of the above Action Pack pages, some areas where I may need support or improvement are:

Based on Action Pack 3-1, my experience with teamwork has been:

Something else you should know about me is:

My expectations and goals for this team effort are:

My time commitments and/or constraints are:

CHART YOUR OWN
TEAM DEVELOPMENT JOURNEY

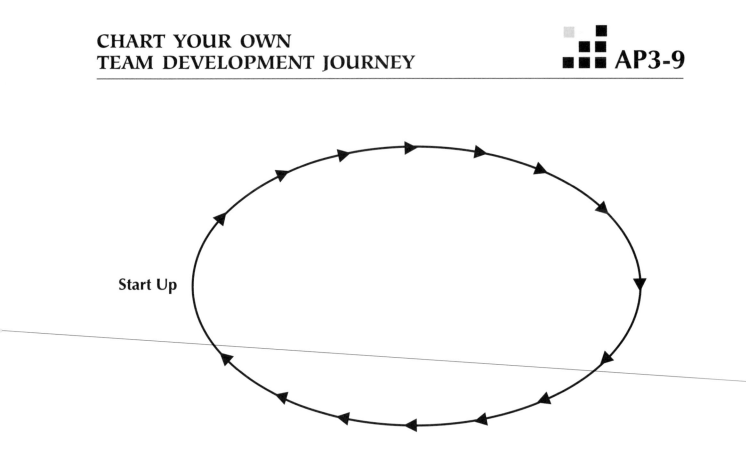

Start Up

Journey Log: Track your team's journey towards unity and productivity. At each meeting, record your feelings about the team and its development. On the diagram above, put the date and a one- or two-word label that describes where your team is on its journey.

Week 1

Week 2

Week 3

Week 4

Week 5

Week 6

Week 7

Week 8

Week 9

Week 10

Week 11

Week 12

Week 13

Week 14

Week 15

CHAPTER 4

Exploring Team Mechanics

What Mechanics Will Help a Team Be Successful?

Time is one of the most valuable resources your members contribute to the team. Each team faces the challenge of using group time efficiently. Experience has shown that successful teams take time to clarify team roles and procedures, confront and resolve conflict, conduct regular self-assessments, and solve problems. Procedures like these lead to efficient team meetings and effective decisions. Understanding some basic team mechanics can ensure that your team uses time efficiently and successfully.

WHAT MECHANICS WILL HELP A TEAM BE SUCCESSFUL?

Several types of mechanics will help your team achieve success. Team roles and team agreements help you know what to expect from one another. Team meeting devices and informational documents keep meetings productive and record important information. Teamwork tools help in decision making and conflict resolution.

Team Role Assignments

Teams have several jobs to accomplish and each member should be clear about his particular role at any given moment. Some groups choose to rotate roles while other groups match team roles to individual strengths and workstyles. Most groups will have some role assignments rotated and other roles assigned permanently. The team should strive to balance the workload while ensuring that the functions for all team roles are covered. On most teams, members will have some overlapping assignments. The following descriptions summarize major responsibilities for some commonly assigned roles.

COORDINATOR OR PRACTICAL MANAGER   This person handles such practical details for the team as reserving meeting rooms, providing written agendas, and arranging for copying or typing of manuscripts. The coordinator provides a central point for communicating schedule changes, absences, or anticipated delays in meeting commitments. He often provides liaison with administrators and others outside the team.

RECORDER   The recorder takes minutes and keeps a processfolio for the team. The processfolio contains team minutes, drafts of individual and group work, time records, team self-assessments, book and material orders, and budget reports. Some groups may choose to identify a separate financial recorder to order materials, submit receipts for reimbursements, and balance the budget.

SUBJECT MATTER EXPERTS   Subject matter experts (SMEs) are information providers. Most teams share this responsibility within their team as individual members become experts in various facets of the content of the theme study. Often a team member brings exceptional expertise to the group and is relied upon as a valued source of information. A member's expertise may be in one of the disciplines integrated into the theme study, curriculum development, instructional strategies, or interpersonal relations. At times, your team may elect to invite outside consultants to share their expertise. For example, a team of experienced teachers might choose to bring in a university professor with knowledge of the latest instructional strategies; a team developing a theme on their community might bring in a local historian; or a team of teachers inexperienced in curriculum development might choose to bring in a curriculum consultant.

PRODUCT MONITOR   This person is charged with keeping an eye on the goals and work schedules. This team member monitors the flow of work, the participation of all members, the use of time, and the accomplishment of goals. The production monitor will also clarify tasks and check the quality of finished products, making sure standards set by rubrics or criteria lists are met.

PROCESS MONITOR The process monitor is focused on the team building process. She ensures that attention is given to studying the cycle of change and team development by promoting self-assessment and reflection in these areas. The process manager promotes full discussion of these issues by questioning, challenging, and probing.

ENCOURAGER As a team, you may be tempted to focus on the work ahead and on unresolved issues. The encourager's responsibility is to remind the team of its accomplishments and progress. His role includes providing encouragement to both the team and individual members. The encourager guarantees that celebrations are planned and some favorite activities are included on meeting agendas. Many teams enjoy shared activities such as reviewing theme-related literature, creating teaching materials, or even browsing in libraries together. Generating activity ideas as a team may also be fun and rewarding. An effective encourager intersperses these motivating activities throughout the team work schedule.

TEAM LEADER A team leader may come from within the team or be a resource person in the school, such as the principal or curriculum specialist. An outside consultant on integrated curriculum development or team development might also be designated the leader. In a university setting, the team leader would typically be the class instructor who is guiding the curriculum work. However, teams may find that they must either share this role or designate one of their members as leader. If a team leader is assigned, his role should be clearly that of a facilitator, enabling the group to become self-directed and productive. The control for the curriculum development process and product must remain with the team. The job of the leader is to keep the team on track and keep meetings running productively. The leader generally starts and ends the meeting. Rather than dictating or making decisions for the team, she leads the group toward consensus and problem resolution.

Use Action Packs 4-1 to 4-8 to brainstorm the exact functions for each team role represented on your team. Then brainstorm words describing the attributes and expected behaviors of a person in that role. These activities will help you clarify the roles important to your team. Figure 4.1 provides an example of this activity for the role of encourager. Use Action Pack 4-9 to keep track of your team's assigned roles.

Team Agreements

Every team needs strategies to deal with the inevitable frustrations and predictable trouble spots associated with teamwork. Professional educators may be tempted to assume that they need no special devices to

Figure 4.1   *Functions, Attributes, and Expected Behaviors of an Encourager*

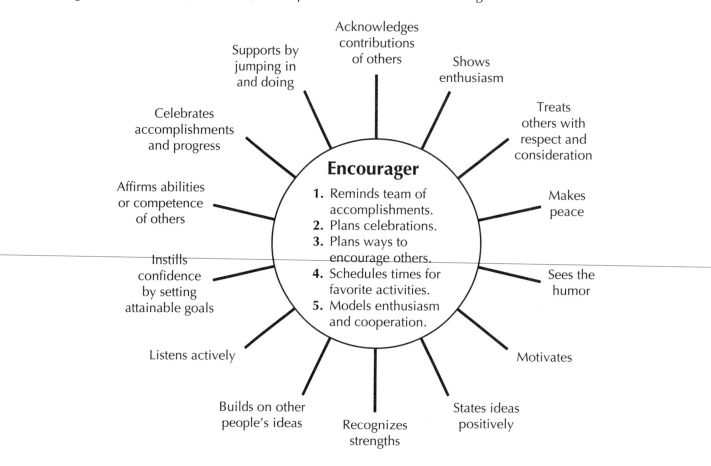

help them work productively and cooperatively. Sometimes teams seem to function well in an informal manner. However, even within the best of teams, misunderstandings can occur that could have been prevented by some organized procedures. One of the major trouble spots is the use of meeting time. Without advance planning, meeting time can be unnecessarily time consuming and nonproductive. In the end, clarifying team expectations saves much time and conflict. The goal for your team should be to provide enough structure to maximize your productivity without sacrificing flexibility and creativity.

One outstanding device for preventing misunderstandings and interpersonal problems is the team agreement. This is a list of ground rules and team expectations generated by members after sharing some personal experiences and information. Team agreements are generally written after the first two or three team meetings. A team agreement brings into the open individual expectations for the team and its members from the perspective of preventing potential difficulties and misunderstandings. Every item on the agreement should have the consensus of the entire team. A team agreement should be viewed as a living document that can be modified as members gain knowledge of one another and the team process. Your team agreement should address a variety of issues. Some team agreements focus only on interactions during meetings while others address larger issues, including the time and work expectations for each team member. We recommend focusing your team agreement around the five areas of concern shown in Figure 4.2: (1) Establishing time and work expectations, (2) Keeping commitments, (3) Creating a risk-free environment, (4) Building on individual strengths, and (5) Developing team unity.

TIME AND WORK EXPECTATIONS   A potential trouble spot is the unfair division of labor. However, team members should realize that work is rarely divided evenly. Some teachers are willing and able to go far beyond the group's minimum expectations. The team should appreciate and welcome this as an individual choice. A reasonable expectation of time and effort, sufficient to produce a quality product and a quality learning process, should be negotiated by your team. Developing a Theme Box is an activity that can go on indefinitely, and some people are reluctant to end the work. Furthermore, as the team learns more, it always sees potential for revision. For these reasons, your team should agree in advance on a definite ending point. According to our research, first Theme Boxes require between 140 to 160 hours of work. Approximately 20 to 25 of these hours are spent in team meetings with the remaining hours divided among the team members for individual work. In a team of four, each person is essentially committing to approximately fifty to fifty-five hours of work. A commitment of this many hours within a reasonable time span should be agreed upon. These estimates are based on time studies done on teams of both preservice and inservice teachers creating their first Theme Boxes. Our studies have also shown that time commitments are not uniform over the weeks of the project. The middle weeks demand more time from team members than do beginning and ending weeks.

Figure 4.2   *Five Areas of Concern for Team Agreements*

☑	Meeting Time and Work Expectations
☑	Keeping Commitments
☑	Creating a Risk-Free Environment
☑	Building on Individual Strengths
☑	Nurturing Team Unity

Other issues in using time efficiently include beginning and ending meetings on time, staying focused both on the product and the process during team meetings, limiting social and sidebar conversations, and allocating and managing breaks.

> LINDA: *I was a member of a team that had one particular statement in its team agreement saying there would be no socialization or sidebar conversations during team meetings. The team quickly found it was unable to live up to that part of the agreement. When a short defined period at the beginning of the meeting was allocated for socialization, team members were then able to focus on our task and our meetings became more productive. We also found that some of our most creative ideas came from sidebar conversations. However, if these ideas were not shared with the entire team, they were not incorporated into the final product. Our team agreement put a limit on the number of sidebars and required that a synopsis be shared with the entire team. Both of these modifications to our team agreement made it fit our individual members' working styles and meet our team need to use time efficiently.*

Teams write statements like these for their agreements to deal with time and work expectations:

- We will start and end meetings on time.
- We like to visit socially but will limit ourselves to 10 minutes of social conversation at a team meeting.
- We will discuss expectations for time commitments at each phase of our work.

COMMITMENTS   The second area your team should address in its team agreement is keeping commitments. Team development and product development cannot occur if team members do not keep the promises they have made. Areas where commitments are needed include attending and participating in meetings, being prepared for meetings, meeting due dates, and honoring the team agreement. Your team must be able to trust each member to fulfill his commitments to the team and individual team members must be able to trust the team to keep its promises to them. This mutual trust is built on the integrity of individual members which then leads to an overall team with integrity. Statements such as these help clarify commitments:

- We will come to meetings prepared and participate fully.
- We will meet due dates or alert the team in advance if we cannot.
- We will notify the team of any intended absence.

RISK-FREE ENVIRONMENT   Team agreements allow discussion about the treatment of team members. This area is important to most people, especially those who have had negative experiences working in groups in the past. The team should be working towards creating a risk-free environment. To build this environment, a team must discuss and build into the team agreement its approach to the areas of confidentiality, respect, conflict resolution, and support. To create a risk-free environment, include statements like these:

- We will share honest opinions without fear of ridicule.
- We will face conflict openly and work toward solutions.
- We will give each member respect and expect it in return.
- We will share feelings, values, and dreams because confidentiality will be maintained.
- We will encourage and affirm each other.

BUILDING ON INDIVIDUAL STRENGTHS   When working together, a team must find ways to use the strengths of its individual members and actively involve each team member. The first step in this area is getting to know the other members on your team. Learn to recognize and respect the strengths of differing workstyles. Use individual interests and knowledge to teach each other. When everyone contributes in his or her area of strength, compensation for individual or team limitations can be made, making your team stronger. Statements such as these help the team fulfill its potential of maximizing the strengths of individual members:

- We will state our needs and preferences and seek to accommodate the needs and preferences of others as well.
- We will be open-minded to others' ideas.
- We will match strengths and workstyles to the tasks facing the team.

TEAM UNITY   Teams need to actively nurture the potential for unity and cohesiveness. Team agreements can help the team to focus on team development as well as product development through statements like these:

- We will give a helping hand to all group members by sharing information and resources.
- We choose to be assertive, not passively blaming or aggressively insisting on our own way.
- We will not form exclusive alliances within the team.
- We will celebrate accomplishments.

In making team agreements, teams should strive towards setting realistic expectations. Certainly, you may realistically expect that work levels and commitment levels will not always be equal. People's life circumstances, skill levels, and interests are very different. However, minimum commitments should be honored. Another issue some groups may need to address is that competition for credit and recognition hinders everyone's best efforts. Rewards should be shared by the team. Furthermore, there must be an honest attempt to value and use everyone's strengths. Both creative contributions and "nuts and bolts" contributions are essential and valuable. Last, you need to remind yourselves that as professionals you do not necessarily have to like someone to work well with him. Clearly, while team agreements should set high expectations for the group, they must be grounded in reality. Use Action Packs 4-10 and 4-11 to guide your team in negotiating your own team agreement.

Team Meeting Devices

Teams best develop when predictable patterns are established. Establishing a regular meeting time and place is wise because teachers' schedules fill very quickly. Changes to this routine should be kept to a minimum. A predictable format for team meetings is also important. Essential team devices that should be a part of a predictable format for your team meetings include agendas, work schedules with due dates, action assignments, meeting minutes, and team self-evaluations.

AGENDAS   An agenda can be a helpful guide for your team meetings. It lists the areas the team is to address, specific activities it needs to execute, and the order in which these items will be addressed. Without a clear agenda, a meeting is likely to result in something no teacher can afford: wasted time and lost productivity. One goal of an agenda is to balance the team's activities. A team might easily spend an entire meeting perusing resource materials or debating philosophical issues. To achieve balanced team meetings, teams can refer to this list of activities: (1) clarifying goals and standards; (2) brainstorming and generating ideas; (3) organizing ideas; (4) sharing resources; (5) sharing individual research; (6) reporting progress; (7) discussing team building processes; (8) discussing curriculum building processes; (9) providing feedback on individual work; and (10) clarifying assignments.

Some areas, such as providing feedback on individual work and clarifying assignments, will usually be included at each meeting. Over time, the team can address all areas. At every team meeting, one of the final things that should be done is to agree on a tentative agenda for the next meeting. At the beginning of each team meeting, the tentative agenda should be revised to establish the actual agenda.

WORK SCHEDULES WITH DUE DATES   To keep work progressing, work schedules with due dates are essential. When scheduling due dates, we have found it most effective to make commitments in increments. Frequent due dates for small sections of the project keep your team on track more effectively than widespread due dates for major pieces of the project. However, a schedule is only as good as every member's commitment to it. Schedule conflicts happen to everyone and sometimes due dates are missed. As you have no doubt learned from other committee assignments, work that is constantly late or not made available to the group puts goals in jeopardy. Everyone's progress, momentum, and motivation is adversely affected. Therefore, a group member who knows he will be unable to fulfill a commitment should let the team know as soon as possible and be ready to negotiate an alternative plan. Figure 4.3 provides sample work schedules our teams have used for both fifteen-week and five-week curriculum writing schedules.

Using these samples, your team should work on a tentative work schedule for your project including checkpoints and due dates. Like your team agreement, this is a living document and modifications can be negotiated as the team gains more experience with the process.

ACTION OR "TO DO" ASSIGNMENTS   Action assignments or individual work make up about eighty-five percent of a team member's time on the project. Therefore, the scheduling and clarification of action assignments should be an important part of every meeting. Each member should leave the team meeting with a clear understanding of his action assignment and commitments. If assignments are scheduled poorly or due dates are missed, some team members may complete steps and then wait for other team members to catch up. The team project can lose momentum. Try to structure the work so that every team member is moving ahead on some work every week. Clarifying assignments at the end of each meeting is important for two additional reasons. First, everyone on the team may agree that something needs to be done, yet no one feels personally responsible. Thus, the task will not be accomplished or more than one person may work on the task resulting in wasted time and effort. Second, a task may have been initially understood in different ways by individual team members. Clarification at the end of the meeting can help eliminate any communication problems.

MINUTES   Undoubtedly, you have had extensive experience with using minutes to record what happens at meetings. Unlike detailed minutes of more formal meetings, team minutes don't have to be elaborate to be useful. All a team needs are simple notes documenting decisions made, action assignments, accomplishments, ideas for later stages of the project, and tentative agenda items for the next meeting. To make sure that this important job is not overlooked, assign one person to take the minutes at each meeting. Your team may decide to make copies of

Figure 4.3 *Sample Fifteen- or Five-Week Work Schedule*

Checkpoint Products	Due Date (15 week)	Due Date (5 week)
Checkpoint 1	**Week 4**	**Week 1**
Concept Statements		
Guiding Questions		
First Draft of a Content Web		
Checkpoint 2	**Week 6**	**Week 2**
Background Information Reports		
Reference Bibliography		
Glossary		
Final Revisions of Checkpoint 1 Products		
Checkpoint 3	**Week 9**	**Week 3**
Graphic Organizers for Students		
Performance Assessment Descriptions and Goals		
First Three Activities for Performance Assessments		
Beginning Annotated Bibliography		
Initial Order of Literature and Teacher Resources		
Revisions of Checkpoint 2 Products		
Checkpoint 4	**Week 12**	**Week 4**
Complete Performance Assessment with Activities		
Supplemental and Literature-Based Integrated Activities		
Annotated Bibliography of Theme-Related Literature and Teacher Resources		
Description of Teacher-Made Materials		
Final Order of Literature and Teacher Resources		
Revisions of Checkpoint 3 Products		
Checkpoint 5	**Week 13**	**Week 5**
Coversheets for Theme Resource Book		
Teacher-Made Materials		
Final Revisions of Theme Resource Book		
Final Theme Box Assembly and Celebration	**Week 15**	**Week 5**

the minutes for all team members in order to publish action assignments for the next meeting. Team members who must miss a meeting should make arrangements to receive a copy of the team minutes as soon as possible. The minutes will keep them aware of team decisions and progress as well as their individual responsibilities.

Reviewing past minutes helps the team to remember useful ideas, to make sure that all tasks have been accomplished, and to celebrate the progress that has been made.

TEAM SELF-EVALUATION   Teams need to pay attention to the process they are going through as well as to the product they are creating. Self-evaluation is an overlooked area—unless time is specifically allocated and a device established to regularly reflect on your team progress. Your team development may be evaluated in several ways. One simple way is to reflect on the question: Are we working well together? Use the checkpoint reflection form found on Action Pack 4-12 as another way to periodically evaluate your team. Your team might either complete the form individually and then discuss answers as a team or fill the form out together. A third method of evaluation is to use the cycle for change and team development from Action Pack 3-9 as a stimulus for sharing perceptions on the team and its development. If more than one curriculum team is operating in the school, having periodic joint meetings to exchange ideas and experiences on the process of working as teams is extremely helpful.

TEAM MEETING PLANNER   A team meeting planner combines elements from all of the team meeting devices that have just been discussed. This is a valuable tool to build an appropriate meeting format. Figure 4.4 is a sample team meeting planner. Action Pack 4-13 provides a planner for your team to try. After using it once or twice, your team may want to modify this planner to meet your needs or you may want to design your own. Using a team meeting planner ensures that a regular format is established and followed for your team meetings. This routine guarantees that important work and team building are not overlooked.

Using this planner, your team would begin each meeting by silently reading the team agreement to remind members of the commitments they made to the team. At this point, you can review the roles members will be filling for that meeting. If someone is absent, his role can be assigned to another team member. Use Action Pack 4-9 to document any assigned role changes. This Action Pack form is especially valuable to groups where roles are rotated. Now, you can move on to step two of the meeting planner and take a few minutes for each team member to share progress, new ideas, or resources. A few minutes to vent frustrations or celebrate accomplishments at the beginning of the meeting will enable everyone to then focus more fully on the current work. Next, review and report on action assignments from the last meeting. This could be as simple as reporting on ordered books or as detailed as sharing research reports with the rest of your team. This will bring the

Figure 4.4 *Sample Team Meeting Planner*

Use this form to plan and record your team meetings.

Meeting Date: _____

Members Present: _____

_____

1. **Team Agreement and Role Review.** Read agreement silently to review commitments. Make any necessary substitutions or changes to team roles.

2. **Individual Share Time.** Share progress, frustrations, new ideas or resources.

3. **Action Assignment Review.** Report on action assignments from last meeting.

4. **Meeting Agenda.** Review and complete meeting work. Document team decisions.

5. **New Action Assignment Review**

   Action _____ Person Responsible _____ Commitment Date _____

6. **Plan next meeting**

   a. Date, time, & place

   b. List agenda items. Consider allocating time for information sharing, resource sharing, brainstorming, peer editing, and reviewing long-term goals.

7. **Team Meeting Evaluation**

   a. **Put an x on the continuum to represent team's answers.**

	None	*Some*	*All*
Were team members prepared?			
Were action assignments done?			
Did members contribute to the meeting?			
Were different viewpoints respected?			
Were members recognized for their ideas?			
Did members listen actively to each other?			
Did the team manage time efficiently?			
Did members stay on task?			
Were conflicts resolved?			
Was consensus reached on major decisions?			
Were meeting objectives successfully completed?			

   b. **Are there any specific problem areas the team needs to address? Does the team agreement need revision?**

   c. **Complete "journey" chart (Action Pack 3-9) to reflect the team's process.**

   d. **Document the team's accomplishments to celebrate.**

entire team up-to-date on individual assignments and remind everyone of past decisions.

At step four, review the tentative agenda items for this meeting and make any needed adjustments. This part of the meeting is when the new work takes place. For example, agenda items for one meeting could include reviewing theme-related literature, creating rubrics, and engaging in peer editing. At times it may be helpful to plan the amount of time allocated to each agenda item. The recorder should also note any "great ideas" coming up during discussions, even if they are not applicable to the immediate task. Documentation assures that no ideas are lost. Above all, make sure that team decisions are documented. Having the recorder read back the final decision will ensure there are no misunderstandings. At step five, record Action or "To Do" Assignments including the action, team member responsible, and the commitment date. Review these also to ensure that everyone understands his responsibility.

At step six, plan for the next meeting by confirming the date, time, and place and record a tentative list of agenda items. Consider allocating time for information and resource sharing, brainstorming, peer editing, and reviewing long term goals. Finish each meeting by completing the team meeting evaluation. If you find some specific problem areas, revisit your team agreement. If you need to make additions or changes to your agreement, do it now. If you need to schedule time for problem solving at the next meeting, add it to your list of agenda items. Reflect upon your team development progress by working on your journey chart. Finally, take time to list accomplishments the team has made and celebrate your progress.

Team Information Documents

In addition to the information documented on a team meeting planner, teams will want to record other types of information. Most teams will want to document information on time and money spent and also information on standards established for individual members' work.

TIME AND EXPENSE FORMS   Most teams will be held accountable for some recordkeeping. If the school district is reimbursing team members for at least some of the time spent on curriculum development, careful documentation of time may be necessary. Even if time records are not required by the administration, teams can learn a great deal about the process of building theme studies by conducting a self-study of ways that time is spent. Figure 4.5 offers a sample time account card that can be adapted to your situation. To adapt this form, decide on ways to break your time into categories and types of work belonging in each category.

Figure 4.5 *Sample Card to Track Individual Time*

School-Based Curriculum Writing Team Individual Time Tracking Card

Week # _____

Record time in minutes: _____

Browse _____   Research _____

Write _____   Group _____

Edit _____   Create Materials _____

Comments:

Discussing this issue at the beginning of your project will ensure that every team member records his time in a similar way. By recording time each week, members can produce an accurate picture of the time spent and thus divide the labor equitably. This information is valuable for the team, other faculty, and the school administration.

Teams should also have a system for keeping accurate expense records and tracking purchase orders. A team should know at the outset the budget for producing its Theme Box. The team also needs to know what in-kind or donated contributions the district is offering. Related questions immediately arise: Are free duplicating services available? Can we count on secretarial help? How will we laminate materials, make transparencies, and create other media? Will a teacher be reimbursed for materials purchased to create teacher-made materials? What is the budget for books and supplementary teaching materials and how should they be ordered? Forms and procedures developed in advance prevent unnecessary frustrations or disappointments. Action Packs 4-14 and 4-15 are sample budget and inventory forms used to track money and materials. Your team may use these or choose to create its own forms.

RUBRICS AND CRITERIA LISTS   Establishing standards is another area where teams must make decisions early. Communicate clearly your team's definitions and standards for excellence by creating a rubric or criteria list for every part of the theme building project. Criteria lists describe qualities to be measured while rubrics create a picture of relevant qualities at various levels of proficiency. Standards let everyone know minimum levels of acceptability. This is especially important for those parts of the curriculum created individually—no one is left guessing what the group expects. By discussing standards at the beginning, the team can deal with ambiguities and develop greater clarity about the task and the product. The team should view rubrics as tentative and open to adjustments as members get more involved with the task. Rubrics and criteria lists are living documents that should be modified as the team clarifies its vision of the final product. Several sample rubrics and criteria lists are provided throughout this book for various parts of the Theme Box.

Tools for Achieving Goals

Even teams that have created team agreements, established patterns for meetings, and negotiated criteria of excellence for the product need other teamwork tools to help them to be successful and efficient. Learning to brainstorm, divide labor efficiently, and celebrate accomplishments are additional tools to help achieve goals. Figure 4.6 summarizes these tools.

BRAINSTORMING   Brainstorming is an activity that allows the team to tap into its creativity and synergy. Throughout this book, we recommend brainstorming as a valuable strategy for teams building themes and for students studying themes. Brainstorming is ideal for encouraging openness to new perspectives, alternative solutions to problems,

Figure 4.6   *Tools for Achieving Goals*

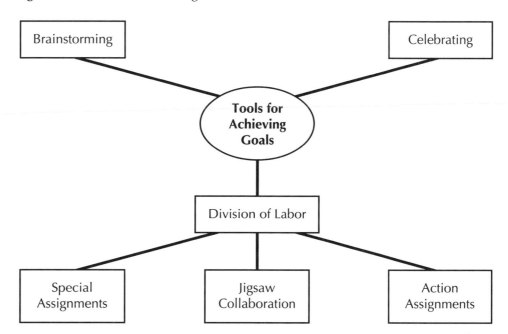

and multiple options. This technique encourages risk taking as well as thoughtful judgment. Figure 4.7 suggests rules for brainstorming your team can adapt or adopt. Basic brainstorming procedures are as follows:

Assign Roles. Assign one person to be the recorder. With one specific person keeping the group list, ideas are less likely to be lost. Of course, the recorder offers ideas as well. Assign another person to act as the expediter, to remind the group not to slip into discussing ideas prematurely, and keep the process moving.

Brainstorm Individually. Start the brainstorming session by silently brainstorming individual lists of ideas. Each member should record as many ideas as possible. If you know prior to a meeting what the topic of your brainstorming session will be, your team members might come to the meeting prepared with personal brainstorming lists.

Brainstorm as a Group. When personal brainstorming lists are completed, the expediter should have someone share one idea. The expediter should allow discussion only when a team member is seeking clarification. The recorder writes down the idea and the entire team focuses attention on that idea. Other team members should then share ideas similar to this proposed idea or suggest new ideas sparked by the first idea. At this point, everyone is reserving judgment on all ideas. It is important to avoid evaluating even your own ideas. Your seemingly inappropriate ideas may lead to the most creative solutions. Continue around the team until the ideas of all the members have been recorded. Even when the group becomes spontaneously excited by a particular idea, the members should continue with the brainstorming. The recorder should safely preserve this favored idea along with all the others and the expediter should prod the group to move on. Remember that the goal of this step is to accumulate a quantity of ideas quickly.

Synthesize and Organize Suggestions. Once a brainstorming activity is completed, teams can edit the list by condensing, refining, and evaluating

Figure 4.7 *Brainstorming Rules*

1. **Accept all ideas.** No analyzing, debating, criticizing, or even discussing. The only exception would be requesting clarification.
2. **Encourage quantity.** The more ideas contributed in a short amount of time, the better. Spontaneous and unusual ideas are encouraged.
3. **Organize ideas at the end.** Once all team ideas have been recorded, they are synthesized, improved, combined, or eliminated altogether.

ideas. Overlapping ideas may be combined or omitted. At this point, ideas should be justified, weighed, and analyzed. The ultimate goal of brainstorming is to evaluate options after viewing issues from multiple perspectives. However, we offer a word of caution: Even when your list has been edited, keep your initial list of ideas. Some teams we have worked with have gone back to their original list to review ideas or when they were unable to come to consensus on the edited list.

Use brainstorming any time you want to spark the creativity or probe the knowledge base of your team. Teams generally find brainstorming to be an exciting activity that validates each person's knowledge and creativity.

DIVISION OF LABOR Learning to divide work equitably using everyone's strengths and skills is a major part of team development. Many teachers have been successful in school and their profession by "doing it all" themselves. Dividing the work of a project can be challenging when working in teams. Some teams make the decision to do all of the work together as a team; however, this greatly increases the amount of time the project will take. Taking time in the beginning to clarify strategies for work division will go a long way to prevent conflict and wasted time. Jigsaw collaboration, "to do" assignments, and special assignments are all ways of dividing the work. Your team may use one or all of the methods explained below to divide your project into manageable individual tasks.

Jigsaw Collaboration. Looking at the overall project or a section of a project and then dividing the big picture into smaller pieces is the basis for jigsaw collaboration. Each team member is assigned one piece. Rubrics or criteria lists set group standards for the work, but each member does the work for his or her piece of the puzzle. When a member completes a rough draft, he shares findings or information with the team; then the team helps with peer editing. Finally, necessary changes are made so that each member's piece fits tightly into the whole product. Teams may decide to divide all the work for a Theme Box this way. Some parts of the Theme Box are usually done by the team collectively; much is done by jigsaw collaboration; while some tasks are divided among the team through special assignments.

Action or "To Do" Assignments. Another way to divide the labor is distributing a list of "to do" assignments with due dates covering one aspect of the project. The team maintains tighter control over the entire process as each section of the project may have two or more team members contributing work towards its completion. Although we would not recommend doing an entire Theme Box in this manner, there may be parts of the Theme Box project that will be handled most efficiently in this manner. For instance, when the group begins browsing to find a central focus for the project, each team member may be assigned a specific place to browse. All information is then brought back to the team for consideration and action.

Special Assignments. The team usually makes special assignments when members have specific valuable skills or access to special technology and resources. Some specially assigned roles could include those of researcher, writer, editor, artist, or computer specialist. Typically, a part of a project will be assigned to the person with these special skills because the team wants the final project to reflect its best efforts. If your team decides to divide the labor in this way, you should monitor closely the amount of time you are asking each team member to contribute. Sometimes one type of work will take significantly more time than another type. If this is true, the team must find ways to balance the amount of time it asks of each team member.

CELEBRATION   Make time to celebrate achievements and progress with your team. We have made acknowledging achievements a part of our team meeting planner because we strongly believe in the need to recognize and reflect on achievements. Team work is hard work, much effort goes into building a Theme Box, and accomplishments should be celebrated. If your team tends to get involved in the work ahead and forgets the celebration, make it a part of your team agreement to "pat yourselves on the back" at checkpoints. This feeling of mutual accomplishment is one of the rewards of team work. At the end of their projects, our teams share their Theme Boxes at an open house celebration with faculty, peers, family, and friends. Consider a concluding celebration of your team work when you formally present your Theme Box to other teachers and administrators in the school.

Tools for Decision Making

Before starting on the Theme Box project, your team has already made many decisions. Just by forming a team and getting ready to work, you have been faced with the need for decision making. But decision making can be a difficult part of team work. Seldom will team members think so much alike that they will always want exactly the same things. In fact, one of the strengths of a team is the diversity of opinions that team members bring to it. Figure 4.8 illustrates techniques your team can use to help make decisions, including voting, building consensus, and resolving conflict.

Figure 4.8 *Tools for Decision Making*

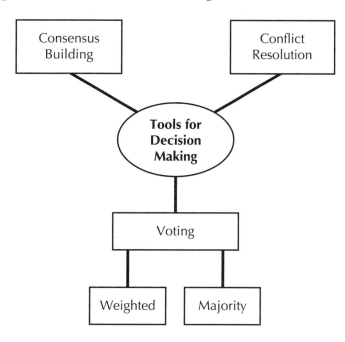

VOTING Living in a democratic society, we are used to the idea of voting with the majority winning. But for teams, we recommend relying on this process only when absolutely necessary. When majority-rule votes are taken, someone must win and someone must lose. For most team issues, there are better ways to come to decisions, such as weighted voting, building consensus, and resolving conflict. With a Theme Box project, some decisions require an unanimous vote. Such is the case when deciding on the central focus of your Theme Box. All team members must agree that they can work enthusiastically with the theme focus.

Weighted voting is useful at times when one or more of your team members feel strongly about a certain idea or decision while others may see two or three decisions that would satisfy them. Using weighted voting, especially to narrow options, can be a valuable tool. Weighted voting can be done in one of two ways. The first way allows each member three votes to use in any way. Team members with strong feelings about a certain option can put all three votes on one option. Those who are happy with two or three options can spread their votes out over those options. In this way, everyone is able to express the strength of his support for an option. The second way allows all members to vote for their top three options. Their first choice receives three votes, second choice two votes, and last choice, one vote. The items with the largest number of votes are then chosen for a short list of options.

Both of these methods allow for more input from the team than a simple one-person, one-vote method. Once your team has created short lists, it can move on to consensus building.

CONSENSUS BUILDING   Using consensus building, a team can reach decisions that everyone can support. While the decision reached may not be an individual team member's top choice, it should be one that every team member finds worthwhile. The first rule in consensus building is to look for areas of agreement rather than areas of disagreement. Often by focusing on these areas of agreement, the team can negotiate a mutually satisfying decision. Ask members to explain the reasons behind their positions. When all participants understand the reasoning or concerns behind positions, they can more easily reach resolutions that meet each member's needs. This is often done by finding ways to combine options. If you reach an option most team members are comfortable with, ask reluctant team members what changes are needed to gain their support. Many times a small change results in a decision that meets everyone's expectations. Once your team thinks it has reached a final decision, poll all team members to make sure they can support the decision. Remember, the question you are asking is not, "Is this your favorite option?" but "Can you support this option?" Consensus building allows everyone on your team to be involved in decision making and feel like a winner.

CONFLICT RESOLUTION   Only a rare team will avoid conflict throughout an entire project. Handling conflict effectively is an important part of team development. Each time a team is able to face and resolve conflict openly and professionally, team members become more comfortable in sharing their honest opinions. Of course, the best method of conflict resolution is prevention. By taking time throughout your project to reflect and work on team development, you will anticipate and eliminate many areas of possible conflict. But when conflict does arise, you must be prepared as a team to respond. The first step in conflict resolution is acknowledging that conflict exists. This should be done with the team as a whole and not handled as a personal meeting between only a part of the team. While allowing the parties of the conflict to explain their sides, it may be necessary to set a time limit. For example, each side may speak for 10 minutes and then have 3 minutes of rebuttal after all sides have spoken. Speakers should reflect on the issues and not on personalities, with only current issues as legitimate topics. Simply airing the conflict may reduce it to a communication failure that can be resolved immediately. If resolution is not reached, once again, as in consensus building, try to find areas of agreement upon which to build. Uninvolved team members can help clarify the viewpoints of contending members and encourage them to find the best solution for the team. In problem solving, we are looking for a win-win solution where all feel they have been heard, understood, and consulted in forming the solution. Use brainstorming to find creative solutions and consensus building to reach a position that all team members can support. Paraphrase the final position to ensure that real consensus has been reached. Each time your team faces and resolves conflict, it will grow in confidence and the ability to build on the diversity of its members.

CONCLUSION

Effective teams organize themselves to conduct efficient meetings, make effective decisions, create quality products, and engage in supportive processes. Several organizational devices support these intentions, including team role assignments, team agreements, team meeting planners, time and expense forms, and rubrics and criteria lists. Effective teams also use a variety of tools for achieving their goals, such as brainstorming, dividing the labor, and celebrating progress and success. Tools for making decisions, including various types of voting, procedures for building consensus, and skills for resolving conflict, are also important to effective teams.

Chapter 5 discusses the first major decision of a curriculum writing team: choosing the focus for its theme study.

Identify the exact functions for the role in the circle. Then brainstorm words that describe the attributes and behaviors expected of a person fulfilling this role for your team.

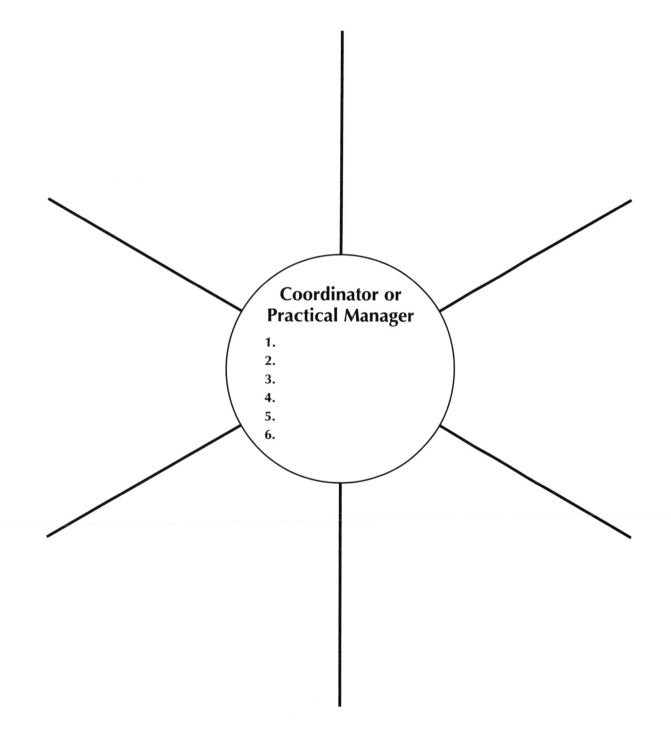

Coordinator or Practical Manager

1.
2.
3.
4.
5.
6.

Identify the exact functions for the role in the circle. Then brainstorm words that describe the attributes and behaviors expected of a person fulfilling this role for your team.

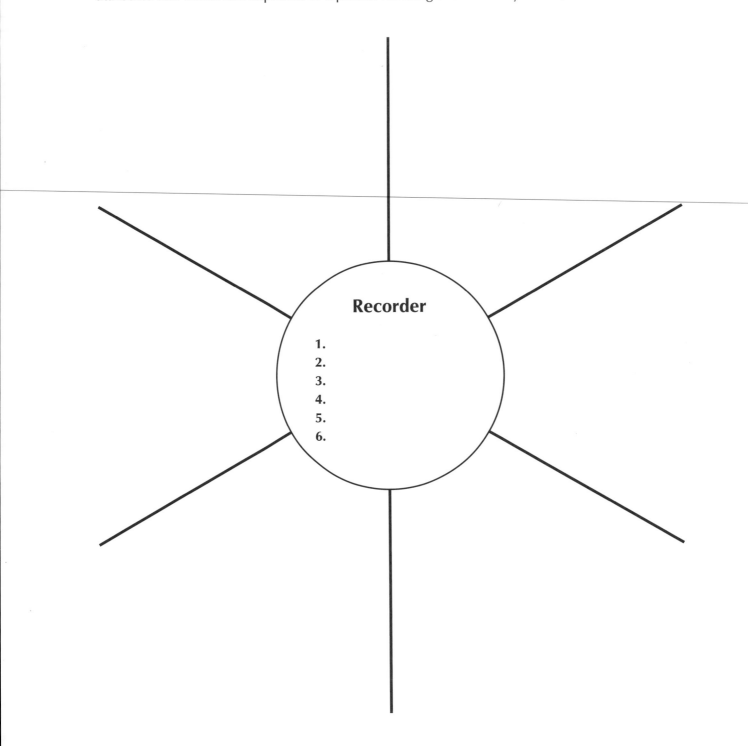

Identify the exact functions for the role in the circle. Then brainstorm words that describe the attributes and behaviors expected of a person fulfilling this role for your team.

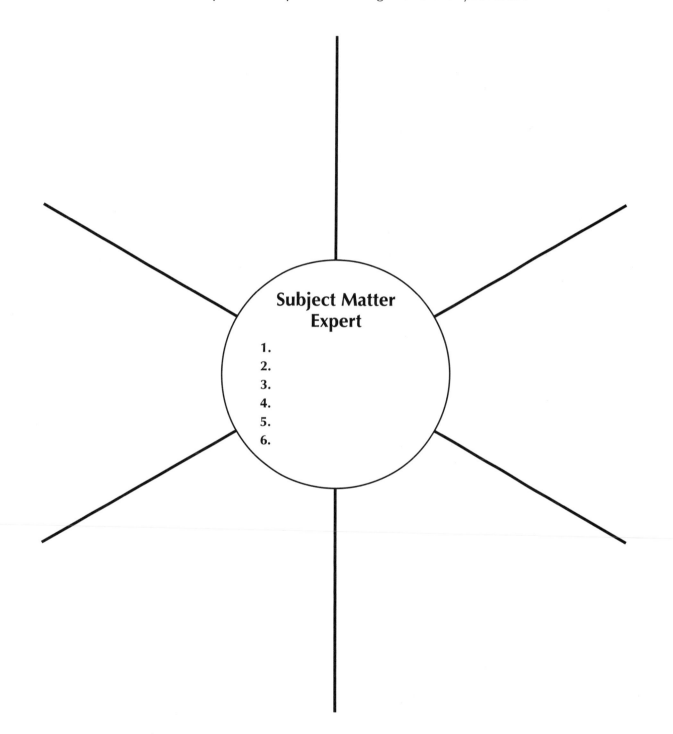

Subject Matter Expert

1.
2.
3.
4.
5.
6.

Identify the exact functions for the role in the circle. Then brainstorm words that describe the attributes and behaviors expected of a person fulfilling this role for your team.

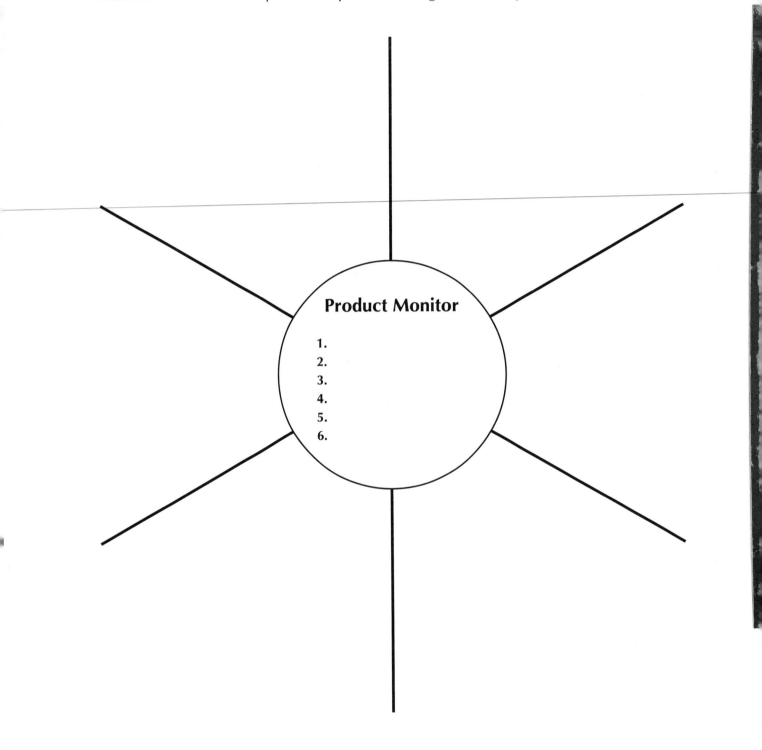

Product Monitor

1.
2.
3.
4.
5.
6.

Identify the exact functions for the role in the circle. Then brainstorm words that describe the attributes and behaviors expected of a person fulfilling this role for your team.

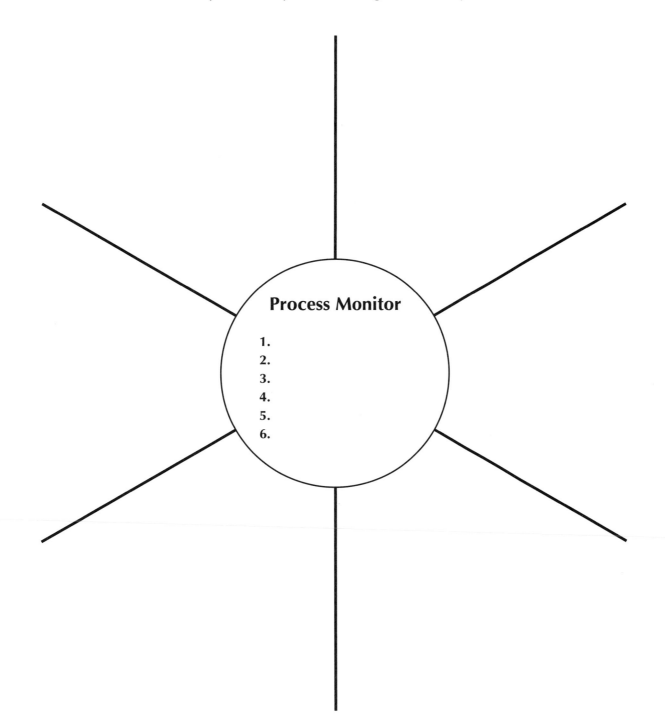

Process Monitor

1.
2.
3.
4.
5.
6.

Identify the exact functions for the role in the circle. Then brainstorm words that describe the attributes and behaviors expected of a person fulfilling this role for your team.

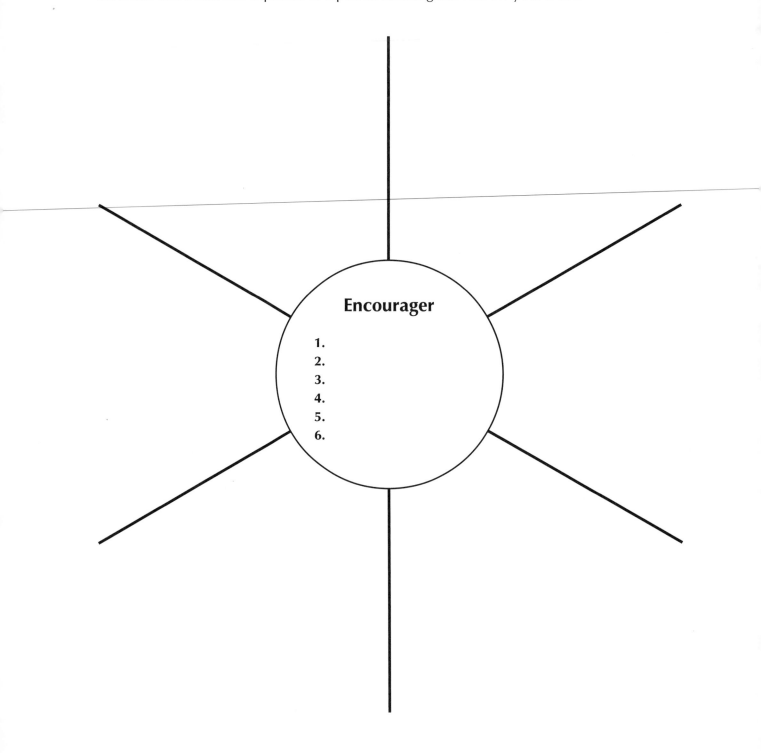

Encourager

1.
2.
3.
4.
5.
6.

Identify the exact functions for the role in the circle. Then brainstorm words that describe the attributes and behaviors expected of a person fulfilling this role for your team.

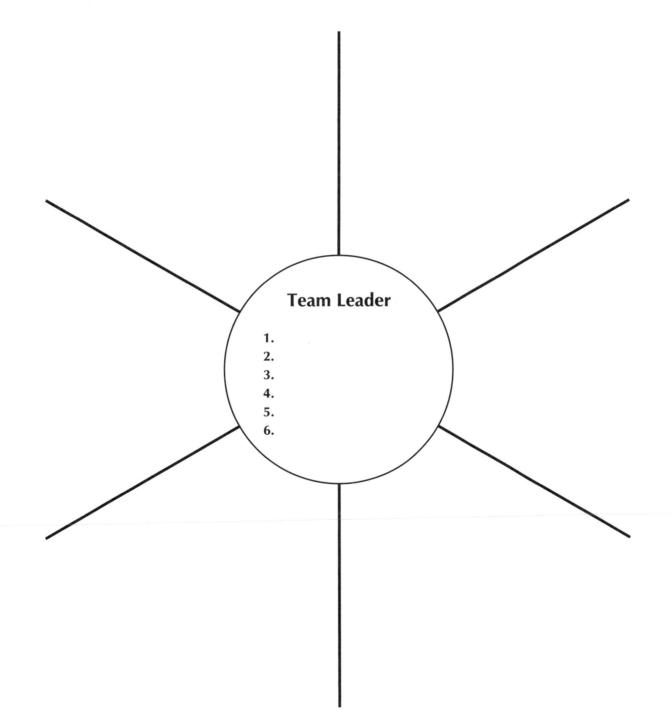

Team Leader

1.
2.
3.
4.
5.
6.

Name a unique role for your team and identify the exact functions for that role. Then brainstorm words that describe the attributes and behaviors expected of a person fulfilling this role for your team.

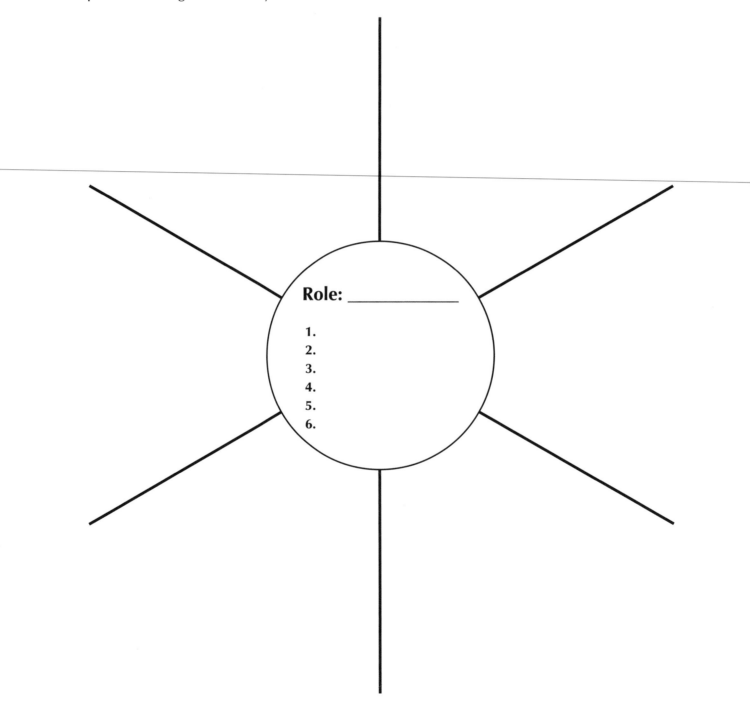

Role: _____

1.
2.
3.
4.
5.
6.

Assigned Member	Team Role	Start Date	End Date	Rotate yes	no
New Assignments or Substitutions					

TEAM AGREEMENT
INDIVIDUAL PREPARATION

 **AP4-10**

Your team will formulate an agreement that provides for team interaction. To prepare for this task individually, review Action Pack 3-1. Consider ways to avoid repeating negative experiences from your past. Some issues to consider are listed below:

Meeting Time and Work Expectations: setting minimum time and effort expectations, beginning on time, allocating social and process time, managing break and ending times, staying focused on the product.

Keeping Commitments: keeping due dates, honoring team agreements, coming to meetings prepared, keeping promises.

Creating a Risk-Free Environment: maintaining confidentiality, sharing honest opinions, treating each other with respect, affirming one another.

Building on Individual Strengths: integrating workstyles, using individual interests, matching strengths and styles to tasks, teaching one another.

Nurturing Team Unity: helping one another, sharing information and resources, planning for conflict and decision making, actively involving each team member, celebrating accomplishments.

List your suggested ideas below:

Share and discuss these items with your team and then create a formal team agreement on Action Pack 4-11.

TEAM AGREEMENT

 **AP4-11**

Team Name: _____ **Date:** _____

As a team, we agree:

Modifications or Changes:

Team Signatures:

_____   _____

_____   _____

1. Important Learning: Describe what you learned during this checkpoint. How does this relate to other work you have done? What discussions or activities were most helpful in your learning process?

2. Team Collaboration: What contributions did you make to your team during this checkpoint? How could your group work more effectively? How could team meeting times be more productive? What has worked well for your team? What attitudes are you developing about collaborative work?

3. Important Feelings: Describe your feelings during this checkpoint. Include your feelings about both your product and the process of curriculum development. Include both frustrations and feelings of accomplishment. What attitudes are you developing about your commitment to excellence?

4. Reflections and Guide to Future Work: What would you change if you had the opportunity to do the work in this checkpoint over again? What questions do you have *now*? What is your plan for getting the information to answer these questions?

TEAM MEETING PLANNER

 **AP4-13**

Use this form to plan and record your team meetings.

Meeting Date: _____

Members Present: _____

_____

1. **Team Agreement and Role Review.** Read agreement silently to review commitments. Make any necessary substitutions or changes to team roles.

2. **Individual Share Time.** Share progress, frustrations, new ideas, or resources.

3. **Action Assignment Review.** Report on action assignments from last meeting.

4. **Meeting Agenda.** Review and complete meeting work. Document team decisions.

5. **New Action Assignment Review**

Action   Person Responsible   Commitment Date

6. **Plan next meeting**

   a.   Date, time, & place

   b.   List agenda items. Consider allocating time for information sharing, resource sharing, brainstorming, peer editing, and reviewing long-term goals.

7. **Team Meeting Evaluation**

   a.   **Put an x on the continuum to represent team's answers.**

	None	*Some*	*All*
Were team members prepared?			
Were action assignments done?			
Did members contribute to the meeting?			
Were different viewpoints respected?			
Were members recognized for their ideas?			
Did members listen actively to each other?			
Did the team manage time efficiently?			
Did members stay on task?			
Were conflicts resolved?			
Was consensus reached on major decisions?			
Were meeting objectives successfully completed?			

   b.   **Are there any specific problem areas the team needs to address? Does the team agreement need revision?**

   c.   **Complete "journey" chart (Action Pack 3-9) to reflect the team's process.**

   d.   **Document the team's accomplishments to celebrate.**

BUDGET REPORT

Date	Item	Amount	Remaining Budget
	Starting Budget Amount		$

INVENTORY TRACKING FORM

 AP4-15

Item	Type*	Date Ordered	Date Rec'd

*B   = Books   M = Music
BB = Bulletin Board   TR = Teaching Resources
C   = Charts   V = Videos
G   = Games

CHAPTER 5

Choosing a Theme

GUIDING QUESTION

How Do You Choose a Focus for a Theme Study?

Every theme study is built around a central idea, called a theme focus or hub. Choosing a focus for a theme study can be perplexing at times. There are endless valuable possibilities, and many school districts have no set requirements for exact themes to be taught. While choosing can be difficult, many teachers find the array of choices to be one of the most delightful aspects of theme building. Sometimes a theme chooses you rather than you choosing a theme.

> DOROTHY: *While I was visiting in Arizona for several weeks, I happened to be shopping in a small cardstore. As I was browsing, I noticed a section of children's books. It took only a few minutes for me to realize that I had in front of me a carefully chosen selection of children's fiction and nonfiction on the American desert. The beautiful books and the learning opportunities they suggested called to me. As I checked out with my eight "must have" selections, the owner told me of her delight in searching for excellent books on the desert. I left the store knowing a theme study was born and my travels would have even greater purpose.*

HOW DO YOU CHOOSE A FOCUS FOR A THEME STUDY?

Usually your curriculum team will systematically consider theme options and determine which ones seem the most beneficial for your students. This chapter presents considerations for selecting a theme focus when your team is free to consider a wide variety of options. First, a team must determine what theme focus category it will use.

Choosing a Focus Category

Before exploring specific theme choices, the team must decide on a type or category of focus to organize the theme study. This category choice will guide the team to different sets of specific theme options. The team can also make better use of the many resources on thematic teaching that are specific to one focus type. Six types of theme focus categories are offered for consideration: literature, topic, abstract concept, event, problem, and position.

LITERATURE THEMES   The focal point for this type of theme study is a single piece of literature, such as *Frederick,* by Leo Lionni (1973), or a set of related literature pieces, such as *Aesop's Fables.* Literature-based themes usually emphasize connections to the language arts. In addition to studying elements of the story itself, connections can be made to all of the language arts by including activities in reading, creative writing, drama, and listening. Some literature-based themes develop connections to other disciplines. For example, a theme study based on *Frederick* would likely include discussions and activities about the varied contributions of all community members. A theme study based on *Aesop's Fables* could provide connections to social studies with research projects about Aesop's life and Ancient Greece. Also appropriate to these themes would be visual art, photography, or music activities from the creative arts disciplines.

TOPIC THEMES   Most topical theme studies address content in the science, social studies, or health areas. However, each study should cross discipline lines. For example, learners studying the solar system might engage in reading, writing, research, creative arts, and mathematical applications as they investigate concepts related to space. Other examples of topic hubs are "whales," "transportation," "the tundra," and "medieval life." Many teachers make a concerted effort to supplement topical investigations with quality literature. A challenging alternative is to teach the chosen topic only through literature, an approach called a "literature-infused" unit (Allen & Piersma, 1995).

ABSTRACT CONCEPT THEMES   For older students, abstract concepts work well as theme hubs, either by themselves or in conjunction with a topic. Examples of such concepts might include "differences," "cycles," and "survival." Erikson in an ASCD videotape (1997) suggests that abstract concepts serve as a lens through which topic hubs can be viewed. When combined with topics, the focus of a theme study might become "differences in ethnic traditions," "life cycles of plants," or "survival of freedom."

EVENT THEMES Important events in the students' lives can be an effective organizing focus. Themes can be derived from producing or attending a play, following the Olympics, or participating in a community celebration. Other events, whether historical, current, or future, may be appropriate for theme investigations if they are relevant, interesting to the learners, and suitable for in-depth, interdisciplinary study.

PROBLEM THEMES Unlike themes taking a position, those focusing on real-life problems are open-ended, having no single clear solution. The hub of a problem-oriented theme is best written as a question. The problem may be global, such as "What can be done about world hunger?," or as specific as a perplexing question posed by a student, "Why don't the animals in our woods die in the winter?" Students pursue solving or at least reflecting on the chosen problem, while freely crossing disciplines. Teachers look for authentic ways for learners to apply skills, processes, and strategies to the particular problem.

POSITION THEMES This focus type takes a stand or point of view that can be challenged or supported. For example, sixth graders might study the position: "Our country, its leaders, and its symbols deserve respect." Another possibility is: "People must assume greater responsibility for endangerment of species and ecological imbalances." In this type of theme study, students are encouraged to follow their investigations wherever they may lead, which is inevitably across discipline lines. Efforts to integrate all disciplines or even a specific set of disciplines is discouraged in favor of following the naturally occurring integration.

Finding Specific Theme Focus Possibilities

Once the team has chosen a focus category, they are ready to generate some specific theme possibilities. Several considerations will yield good candidates for themes.

CONSIDER CURRENT CURRICULUM The first place to look when considering theme possibilities is at the current curriculum. This starting point is particularly important if the team is concerned about an already overcrowded curriculum. By mapping the current curriculum according to the content taught in each subject area each month, the team can eliminate repetitions and optimize natural connections (Jacobs,

1989, 1997). Thoughtful analysis will identify content from several disciplines that can be effectively integrated.

CONSIDER QUALITY LITERATURE   If the team will be designing a literature-based thematic unit, then the most obvious way to begin is by creating a list of appropriate, high quality literature. One consideration in building the list is to identify the literature loved by students and their teachers. If you teach in elementary education, expand your knowledge of children's favorites by consulting *The Reading Teacher*. The October issue of each year includes an annotated bibliography of books selected by children as their favorites. To find other books, review lists of award-winning books and those highly recommended in literature reviews.

Worthwhile literature is an important part of any theme study, not only those that are literature-based. For example, if you have decided to pursue a science or social studies topic for your theme, you might consult the March issue of *Science and Children* and the April/May issue of *Social Education* for annotated bibliographies of outstanding books in these disciplines published within the last year.

CONSIDER CURRENT HAPPENINGS   Theme studies are meant to be meaningful and relevant. Nothing is more relevant than the students' current world. One way to capture immediacy is to use emerging interests as the basis for theme studies. Teachers noticing their students' fascination with the insects on the playground or an upcoming space launch can respond by initiating study of these phenomena. While some of these theme studies may be spontaneous, many types of current happenings can be anticipated and prepared for in advance. Even the progression of the calendar with changing seasons, celebrations, and special remembrances offers theme possibilities relevant to students' lives. Upcoming events such as national elections or cultural events would fall into this category. Other theme possibilities might be suggested by taking advantage of the best of the permanent and special exhibitions of local museums. One teacher we know tracks all of the traveling exhibitions at local museums.

> DOROTHY: *A docent at a large local museum of natural history spoke with me about different groups of students coming through the museum. This museum educator explained that some groups are engaged in studies for which one or more exhibitions are a valued resource. Their visits have clear and engaging purposes. The docent shared that the experience is totally different for groups visiting the museum with no preparation, no critical questions to ask, and no clear need to find information. The experiences of this docent led her*

to believe that unprepared students gain only general impressions while students engaged in theme studies notice details supporting in-depth understanding.

In addition to these types of current happenings, many schools have visiting authors and resource experts. Preparing for their visits may suggest some exciting themes for in-depth study.

CONSIDER THE INTERESTS AND EXPERIENCES OF TEACHERS AND PARENTS Many students have had their minds opened to new interests when a teacher or parent shared his passion for a place, topic, hobby, or area of study. Teachers using a thematic approach as one model of teaching can and should consider theme focus possibilities based on their travels and ongoing interests. Likewise, many of your students' parents will have valuable experiences, travels, hobbies, or areas of expertise to share. Motivating students to learn is not difficult when introduced to topics that fascinate the important adults in their lives.

CONSIDER THE UNIQUENESS OF YOUR COMMUNITY The immediate environment in which students are living every day is interesting to them and presents many opportunities for in-depth study. To take advantage of this rich resource, reflect on these questions: What are the natural resources, industries, cultural heritage, important historical places, and events in our area? What problems does our community face? What makes our community special? What roles in community life are played by the families of those we teach? Theme building can help teachers and students to find the answers to these important questions.

CONSIDER THE STRONG INTERESTS OF STUDENTS As teachers, we often think that we know what is interesting to our students. However, most of us would profit from a more deliberate, objective survey of students' interests. Asking learners about their interests and then listening carefully with an open mind is one of the best ways to find out. You may unexpectedly discover your particular group of fifth graders loves to talk about pets, or your middle school group is fascinated with Ancient Egypt. Even without asking them directly, student interests can be researched in many ways. First, listen carefully to their stories, conversations, and questions. Next, read their body language. When do their eyes light up? What worries them or perplexes them? Paying attention to the types of books that students select when given free choice is another powerful indicator. Finally, check with other teachers, media specialists, parents, and museum educators to see what they have noticed about learners' interests.

Choosing a Theme Focus

Once a team has chosen the type or category of focus to organize its theme study, the next step is to select a specific theme focus. A three-step process will lead to the best choices for a theme focus: (1) generating possibilities, (2) evaluating possibilities, and (3) reaching consensus.

GENERATING THEME POSSIBILITIES   When generating theme possibilities, the goal is to create a long list including many ideas beyond those immediately obvious to you. We recommend five ways of generating theme possibilities: mapping, observing, consulting, browsing, and brainstorming. We offer procedures for generating these possibilities in Action Packs 5-1 to 5-13. Teams may choose from among the activities described on these pages the ones that they find most profitable for producing an interesting and varied list of theme focus possibilities. While not every activity for generating theme possibilities needs to be pursued, we recommend a wide variety of approaches.

> DOROTHY: *A team of teachers was certain it wanted to develop a Theme Box on an interesting place. After doing some brainstorming, the group settled on a theme study of the tundra. The team members believed it was not necessary to do browsing or consulting for additional possibilities since they were so satisfied with the focus choice. After they were well into their work, however, they were browsing through catalogues and encountered interesting materials on Ancient Egypt, a topic they found highly interesting. All in the group were disappointed they had not considered this possible focus. Their experience reinforced for us the importance of using a wide variety of activities for generating theme possibilities.*

Mapping. Mapping the current curriculum is an excellent way to generate theme possibilities. This technique provides the writing team with information on what, when, and where content is taught. Jacobs (1997) outlines the following effective procedures for curriculum mapping. First, determine the grade levels to be included in your curriculum map. Then have each teacher in these levels complete a month-by-month chart using the school calendar. This chart will include the important content and units of study being taught in each subject. It is essential that "the taught curriculum" is charted rather than the official district or school plan. The team compiles this data and analyzes it for redundancies, gaps, and natural connections. With this larger perspective, it often becomes apparent that the content from two or more subject areas can be effectively integrated into one theme study if taught concurrently. Additionally, gaps in the current curriculum will become obvious, suggesting potential theme studies to the team. Curriculum mapping is productive not only for generating theme possibilities, but for monitoring the variety of theme studies and units within the school. This second purpose will be explored in Chapter 9. Action Packs 5-1 and 5-2 provide a curriculum mapping guide.

Observing. Observing students to learn about their interests is a productive and enjoyable activity. We recommend that teachers keep on hand a "noticing notebook" for recording information about interesting or perplexing topics. Key times for gathering this kind of information are when students choose activities or books, engage in informal conversations, or participate in sharing circles. Action Pack 5-3 provides an observation guide to record your findings about student interests.

In addition, the team should observe what is happening or will be happening in the school, community, nation, or world that could be interesting to students. Preparing students in some way for significant events is important. A theme study is one possibility. Even a regularly scheduled event such as a trip to a museum is enriched by preparation. For help in observing current happenings of interest to students, use Action Pack 5-4.

Consulting. Observations are productive, but direct requests for recommendations will also lead to some exciting alternatives. Fellow teachers are excellent sources of theme ideas. Museum educators and media specialists can offer unique perspectives on young people's interests. Community leaders often have good ideas about what learners should know about their town or region. Parents and students themselves will have excellent suggestions to make. Action Packs 5-5 to 5-8 will help guide your consulting activities.

Browsing. Teachers and other educators experienced in thematic teaching are constantly publishing theme resource materials. Teachers' stores, bookstores, and educational catalogues are fruitful resources to browse for theme ideas and initial assessments of available materials. Additionally, a team might conduct a library survey by checking several indexes and periodicals providing annotated bibliographies of age-appropriate books. Be sure to skim through various textbooks, as well as state and local curriculum guides, to determine what content other curriculum writers consider important. When available, the recommendations of learned societies setting national standards are worth reviewing. Use Action Packs 5-9 to 5-11 to assist you with your browsing activities.

Brainstorming. Naturally, many of your team members will come to early team meetings with some theme ideas in mind. Preserving these ideas as well as collecting other possibilities for themes is a good practice. You should first record your ideas individually and then follow the rules of brainstorming to generate other ideas with your team. Avoid committing yourselves prematurely to a favored idea until you have given serious consideration to other possibilities. If you prefer an open-ended type of brainstorming, use Action Pack 5-12 to record your list.

Categories are sometimes helpful in ensuring that the team considers a full range of possibilities. One way to organize your brainstorming in categories is to list your theme ideas on the brainstorming organizer provided in Action Pack 5-13. Categories suggested earlier in this chapter can provide a method of organizing your brainstorming. Your team may have its own category ideas. Some of your theme ideas may be listed in more than one category. To prompt your thinking as you complete this Action Pack, use the following questions:

1. Established educational goals and current curriculum demands:
   What do we believe students of this age should be learning?
   What do national learned societies recommend?
   What are the curricular goals of the state and district?
   What is the content of our current curriculum?
2. Current happenings:
   What current events would intrigue students?
   What upcoming events have potential for important learning?
   Who will be visiting our school, our area, or our local museums?
   What outstanding achievements have been made by local people and groups?
3. Strong interests of students:
   What have we learned about the interests of the students we have observed and interviewed?
   What interests have been indicated by parents and other educators?
   What do we know about the interests of learners of this age?
4. Uniqueness of the community:
   How is this community different from others?
   What features and activities interest visitors to this area?
   What should students understand about their home area and its people?
5. Teachers' and parents' interests and experiences:
   What kind of learning excites us?
   What interesting places have we visited?
   How could our hobbies or passions enrich student understanding?

What are some of the unique experiences, hobbies, and interests of our parent resources?
6. Literature:
   What great literature comes to mind that is age appropriate and loved by both students and teachers?
   What literature has received awards and recommendations?

EVALUATING OPTIONS   Any team writing, teaching, and revising one specific theme study commits itself to living with that focus for an extended period of time. Therefore, every member of the team must be enthusiastic about the theme chosen. Each team member must strive to be both open-minded and forthcoming in discussions about possible themes. A passive reaction from a group member should not be interpreted as agreement. Following the organizing activity, the group should review its list of possibilities, combining or eliminating duplicated or similar themes. Then group members should propose their favorites for closer evaluation. This short list of favorites should be evaluated for educational value, interest to students and teachers, available resources, appropriateness for a thematic approach, appropriate breadth, and the potential for connections to other theme studies. Use Action Pack 5-14 to complete the evaluation of your short list.

Reflect on the Educational Value. Some teachers may have a great deal of academic freedom in choosing themes to study. But in reality, most teachers face an overcrowded curriculum and time limitations. Therefore, teaching teams consider the potential of any theme for meeting mandated outcomes and skills and for fitting the theme into the entire scope of the curriculum. National standards prevail in various disciplines, and local guidelines must be observed. You can also make decisions about educational value when you take into account your knowledge of human development and developmental appropriateness. Another determining factor is the extent to which the theme allows for integration of language arts and math skills, two highly valued areas in the elementary and middle school. Clearly, all teams of teachers should spend time on these questions: What is truly important, worthwhile knowledge for these students? Does this theme support the construction of valuable and lasting knowledge?

DOROTHY: *Recently members of a curriculum writing team became excited about developing a Theme Box on a strong interest of theirs: camping. However, when they reflected on the educational value of their choice, they became concerned about the lack of substance. After some deliberations, they decided on the focus of "Our National Parks: A Camping Trip," which proved successful.*

Reflect on the Interest Level of Students and Teachers. An interdisciplinary theme study can be an immensely satisfying and motivating learning experience for students and teachers alike. This motivation is best fueled by a lively interest in the theme focus. Thematic teaching cannot fulfill its optimal potential unless considerable attention is given to the interest of both students and teachers in the theme focus.

Check the Availability of Resources. Sufficient numbers of quality resources are essential for thematic studies. Therefore, you should review the available resources before committing to a particular theme. Learners deserve great literature and require multiple sources of information at an appropriate reading level in order to do research. Teachers should also consider the community resources available, such as speakers, experts, museums, and field trips. Consulting with the school media specialist is a good starting point in determining the availability of needed resources.

Determine the Best Way to Teach the Topic. Not every good topic is best taught as an interdisciplinary theme study. Ask if this topic lends itself naturally to in-depth investigations that cross disciplinary lines. Furthermore, determine whether active learning and open-ended problem-solving activities are appropriate for this topic.

Evaluate the Breadth. Theme development becomes frustrating when a theme choice is either too broad or too narrow. Scarcity of resources, lack of connections, and lack of related global concepts are good indications of an excessively narrow theme choice. We have found that workable themes usually have about four to seven well-developed concept statements. Some teachers may think that the best approach would be to work with very broad themes. In fact, too many resources and too many important aspects can make units overwhelming. Certainly, the amount of time you have available to spend on a theme has an impact on its scope. Deciding if a topic is too broad or too narrow is best postponed until the team has completed its research. Keeping flexible will allow a team to see productive ways to adjust the breadth of the topic choice.

Consider Possible Theme Connections. A school might wish to consider the option of developing a set of related themes. When curriculum developers follow this approach, they consider not only the connections within a theme, but also possible connections among themes. For example, when students study a variety of geographic regions in an intellectually responsible way, they will learn certain broad generalizations applying to every geographic region studied. The following is a set of broad concept statements applying equally to regions such as the rain forest, the African grasslands, the American desert, the tundra, and the temperate forests.

A. The (rain forest, African grasslands, etc.) is a geographic region with its own climate, land forms, and natural resources.
B. All living and nonliving parts of (the rain forest, grasslands, etc.) are linked together in a naturally functioning ecosystem that must be preserved.
C. A wide variety of plant life is uniquely adapted to the (desert, temperate forest, etc.).
D. Animal species living in (the tundra, the desert, etc.) are survivors of natural selection and are adapted to the environment.
E. The (African grasslands, tundra, etc.) is home to a diversity of people whose cultures have been influenced by the climate, land forms, and natural resources.

Figure 5.1 shows a sample hierarchical graphic organizer designed to reflect possible theme connections for a theme study on the African Grasslands. The important conceptual structure among these themes could be developed in several ways. Students in the same classroom could study two or more geographic regions emphasizing the global understandings, or different groups within the same class might become experts on different geographic regions. Teachers and staff might decide to do a school-wide theme on geographic regions with different groups or grades studying the same concepts as they apply to different regions.

Figure 5.1   *Possible Theme Connections for a Theme Study on the African Savanna*

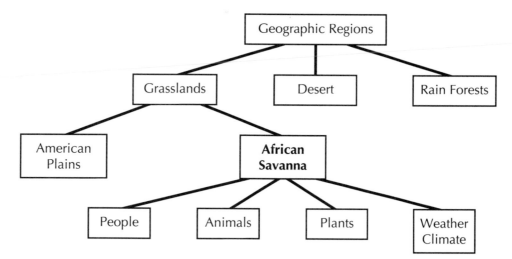

Figure 5.2   *Sample Theme Connection Hierarchy*

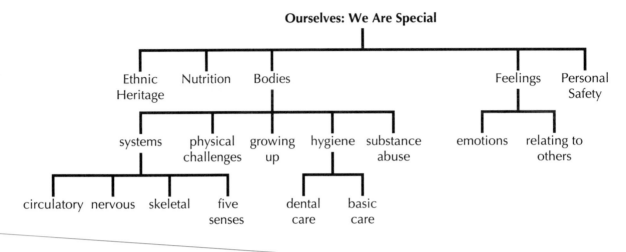

Classes could share with one another how the essential understandings apply to their particular region. For example, a school-wide theme of geographic regions might involve fourth graders studying the rain forest, third graders studying the American desert, and second graders studying the African grasslands. Within the second grade, some classrooms could be studying the American plains while other classrooms study the African savanna. Students would investigate concepts related to ecosystems, people, animals, plants, climate, landforms, and resources

Figure 5.3   *Sample Theme Connection Hierarchy*

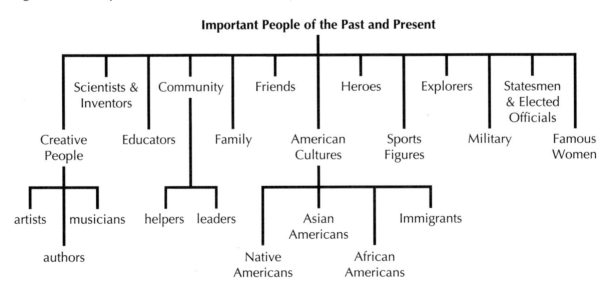

Figure 5.4 *Sample Theme Connection Hierarchy*

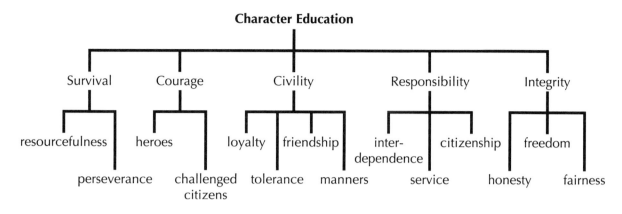

for each geographic region. A prominently displayed graphic organizer connecting the work of all the grades and classrooms could show the differences and similarities that the students have found. Use Action Pack 5-15 to generate possible theme connections for each theme focus you are considering.

Figures 5.2 to 5.6 offer hierarchies of connected theme topics that might be studied school-wide or explored in individual classrooms. The topics mentioned are also ones for which there appear to be adequate

Figure 5.5 *Sample Theme Connection Hierarchy*

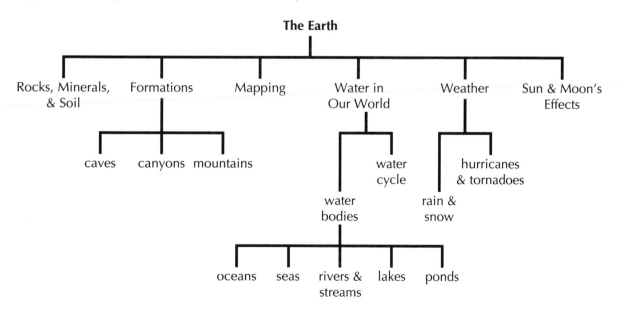

Figure 5.6   *Sample Theme Connection Hierarchy*

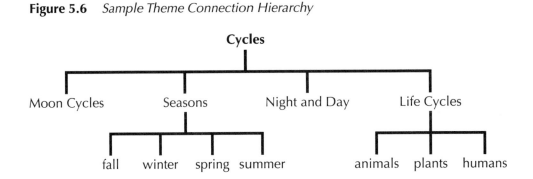

resources available to elementary and middle school learners. These theme ideas are topical in nature. Other hierarchies might be designed to address possible connections between themes that focus on specific pieces of literature, events, abstract concepts, position statements, or problems.

REACHING CONSENSUS   Reaching consensus on a theme focus may be easy, painless, and quick for some curriculum writing teams. Unfortunately, not all groups experience this initial unity. If your group is struggling, you should each try to avoid locking into one favorite choice. Work to stay open to other ideas. On the other hand, do not accept a focus simply to avoid conflict. This is one case where taking a majority vote is definitely not an appropriate decision making approach. Ultimately, this curriculum writing project will require the enthusiastic support of everyone. Consensus must be reached by trying to use differences of opinion creatively. Some groups with whom we work reject their short lists and return to their long lists to further analyze the options. More than one group has chosen a topic that never appeared on its initial long list. In such cases, the final choice was reached by returning to the activities of mapping, observing, consulting, browsing, and brainstorming. The search for an agreeable, valuable theme is worth the time and effort. For the team that is thinking it has reached a final choice, we recommend two final actions. First, survey every team member for enthusiastic verbal support. Second, celebrate the fact your team has made an important step in the theme building process by indulging in some dreaming about the future Theme Box and theme teaching.

CONCLUSION

Choosing a theme is usually the first major decision facing a school-based curriculum writing team. Before the team can identify a specific focus, however, it must choose the type of theme to be planned. The major focus categories are: literature, topics, abstract concepts, events, problems, and positions. Once the team has chosen a category, it can generate specific focus possibilities through mapping, observing, consulting, browsing, and brainstorming activities. The team then evaluates its favorite focus ideas using established criteria. Above all, the team must reach enthusiastic consensus on its focus.

Once the curriculum building team identifies a focus, it must establish parameters for the theme study. These parameters are essential for enabling the theme to have substance and cohesiveness. Chapter 6 describes how the parameters of concept statements, guiding questions, and a content summary are established.

Curriculum Map of Major Topics and Units

Grade_____

Month	Subjects					
Sept.						
Oct.						
Nov.						
Dec.						
Jan.						
Feb.						
Mar.						
Apr.						
May						
June						

After mapping your curriculum, use these questions to guide your analysis.

1. What current content could be effectively integrated in a theme?

2. What current themes are being taught? Could more content subjects be integrated into those themes?

3. What gaps in your current curriculum become obvious?

4. After analyzing your curriculum map, answer the question: What theme topics are suggested by your analysis?

   a.
   b.
   c.
   d.
   e.

Classroom Observed: _____

Date: _____

Observe a class for a day, specifically looking for students' strong interests. Use the questions below as guides for your observation.

1. What did students choose to do with their free time?

2. What topics appeared in students' spontaneous conversations and questions?

3. What books did these students choose to read?

4. Were there any specific activities or topics that excited the class?

5. After observing the students, answer the question: What theme topics are suggested by your observations?

   a.
   b.
   c.
   d.
   e.

Sources: _____   **Dates:** _____

_____   _____

_____   _____

1. Study the national and local news. What topics or events would be of interest to your students and would be profitable to investigate?

2. Study the entertainment sections of local papers. What events, plays, and interesting places suggest possibilities for theme studies?

3. Contact the local Chamber of Commerce for information. What are some upcoming community events?

4. Contact local museums and science centers. What are their most extensive permanent exhibits? What traveling exhibits are planned? What educational programs and services do they offer?

5. After completing these observations, answer the question: What theme topics are suggested by this information?

   a.

   b.

   c.

   d.

   e.

Generating Theme Possibilities
CONSULTING STUDENTS

 **AP5-5**

Students' names: _____ **Students' ages** _____

_____ _____

_____ _____

Dates: _____

Interview two or more students using the questions below as guides or conduct a written survey using these questions.

1. What do you like to do when you have free time?

2. What hobbies or collections do you have?

3. What are some of your favorite places to visit?

4. What kinds of TV shows and movies do you watch?

5. What kinds of books do you like? What are your three favorite books?

6. If you could learn about anything you wanted, what would you study?

7. After interviewing or surveying the students, answer the question: What theme topics are suggested by these consultations?

   a.
   b.
   c.
   d.
   e.

115

CONSULTING WITH TEACHERS, MEDIA SPECIALISTS, AND OTHER ADULTS

 AP5-6

Consultants' names: _____ **Positions:** _____

_____ _____

_____ _____

Dates: _____

Using these questions, interview two or more adults or conduct a written survey of adults who work with children or young adolescents.

1. What have you found to be of the greatest interest to students in elementary and middle schools?

2. What books have you shared with young learners that were enthusiastically received?

3. What do you think are valuable themes for students to study?

4. What topics do teachers and students frequently ask about?

5. After interviewing or surveying the adults, answer the question: What theme topics are suggested by these responses?

   a.
   b.
   c.
   d.
   e.

Generating Theme Possibilities
CONSULTING WITH PARENTS

 **AP5-7**

Parent's Name: _____ **Children's ages** _____

Date: _____

Using these questions, conduct a written survey of the parents of your students.

1. What hobbies, talents, or special interests do you have that would interest students?

2. Where have you traveled that you think students should learn about?

3. What are some of your children's special interests?

4. What are some of your children's favorite books?

5. After surveying the parents, answer the question: What theme topics are suggested by these responses?

    a.
    b.
    c.
    d.
    e.

117

Names: _____ **Positions:** _____

_____ _____

_____ _____

Date: _____

Use the following questions as a guide to interview two or more community leaders or conduct a written survey of several community leaders.

1. What special attributes of our community should elementary and middle school students know about?

2. What unique resources does our community have?

3. What are some of the problems our community is currently facing? What is being done about those problems?

4. What are some aspects of your work that students should know about?

5. After completing the interview or survey, answer the question: What theme topics are suggested by these responses?

   a.

   b.

   c.

   d.

   e.

Generating Theme Possibilities

BROWSING TEACHERS' STORES, BOOKSTORES, AND CATALOGUES

Stores Browsed: _____

_____

Dates: _____

1. What published theme studies are available?

2. What trends do you notice in the available supplementary and resource teaching materials?

3. What trends do you notice in the available theme-related literature?

4. After completing your browsing, answer the question: What theme topics are suggested by this material?

    a.

    b.

    c.

    d.

    e.

Library Browsed: _____

Date: _____

1. Consult the following journals for bibliographies of current and favorite
   children's books: March issue of *Science and Children*
      April/May issue of *Social Education*
      October issue of *The Reading Teacher*
   List several books that suggest possible theme topics.

2. List any books that appear in more than one of the above sources. Do they suggest any
   theme topics?

3. Find the library's collections of published units, theme resources, and textbooks. What
   theme materials are available?

5. After completing your library browse, answer the question: What theme topics are
   suggested by this information?

   a.

   b.

   c.

   d.

   e.

BROWSING STATE AND
LOCAL GUIDELINES

 **AP5-11**

Documents Browsed: _____

_____

Date: _____

1. Look through state and local curriculum guidelines. What content is *required* that could be taught thematically?

2. Look through state and local curriculum guidelines. What content is *recommended* that could be taught thematically?

3. After completing your browse, answer the question: What theme topics are suggested by this information?

    a.

    b.

    c.

    d.

    e.

Brainstorming Rules

1. **Accept all ideas**
   No discussion or debate is acceptable.

2. **Encourage quantity**
   Spontaneous and unusual ideas are welcome.

3. **Organize at the end**
   Edit ideas by synthesizing, improving, or eliminating.

Record your individual list of theme possibilities:

Record your team list of theme possibilities:

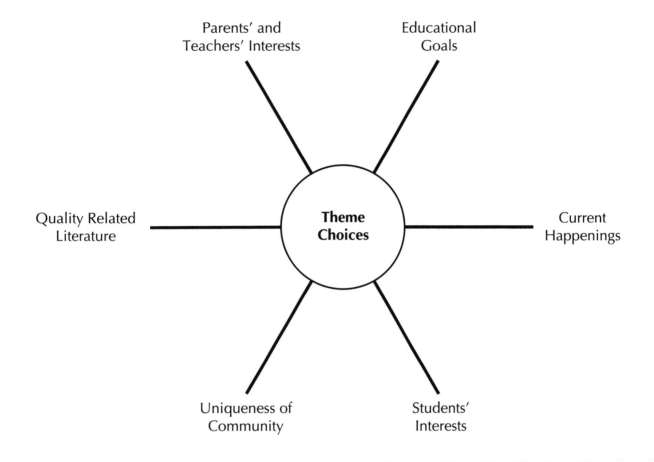

Instructions: Brainstorm theme possibilities using these categories.

Using the following criteria, evaluate your short list of theme possibilities.
Use a scale from one to three, with three being the highest.

1 = Educational Value
2 = High Interest to Students and Teachers
3 = Availability of Resources
4 = Appropriate for Thematic Teaching
5 = Appropriate Breadth
6 = Possible Theme Connections
7 = Total

Theme Focus Possibilities	1	2	3	4	5	6	7

After totaling scores for each theme possibility, your team should make a final decision on its theme focus. The theme focus chosen will not necessarily be the focus with the highest score but should be one of the highest. Reach this decision using consensus building skills from Chapter 4. Every team member must be willing to support your final theme focus choice.

Final Theme Focus:

As a member of this team, I support the theme focus.

Signatures of team members:

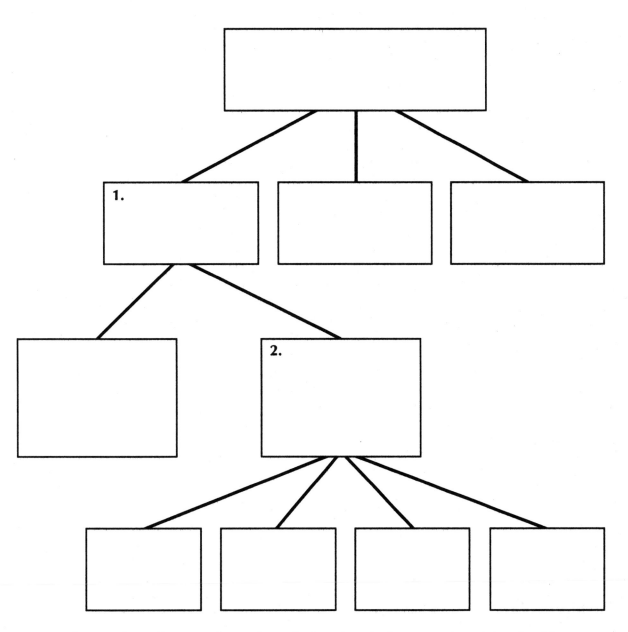

Instructions: Put your theme focus in Box 1 or 2, then complete the web with connecting themes.

CHAPTER 6

Establishing the Parameters of a Theme Study

GUIDING QUESTION

How Do Curriculum Builders Determine What Is Worth Knowing?

Interdisciplinary thematic approaches are ideal for teaching many learning processes and thinking skills. Consequently, some educators might conclude that the content of a theme study is irrelevant so long as learners are becoming creative, critical, and flexible thinkers. However, time in school is short, and in-depth theme studies require a significant time commitment. While theme studies can't be rushed, neither should they waste any valuable learning time. The job of a school-based thematic curriculum writing team is to establish the boundaries of a theme study so that learners focus their time on valuable study while simultaneously learning important processes. An interdisciplinary thematic unit must lead students to conceptually related ideas that will help them better understand their world. Therefore, a question that is constantly before a curriculum writing team is "What is most worth knowing?"

HOW DO CURRICULUM BUILDERS DETERMINE WHAT IS WORTH KNOWING?

Five curricular aspects enable teams to determine what is worth knowing and define the parameters of a theme study: (1) the central focus, (2) the concept statements, (3) the guiding questions, (4) the content summary, and (5) the performance assessments addressing the concept statements and guiding questions. These aspects help curriculum writers and implementing teachers achieve coherent, purposeful theme studies. Within these parameters, teachers and classes have room for much individual choice. Some classroom teachers may choose to develop only some of the content or a selected few concept statements because time is short or their interest is more focused. Figure 6.1 illustrates the five key parameters serving as the framework for a theme study.

Chapter 5 clarifies the issues surrounding the process of identifying a theme focus. The process for creating effective assessments is explained in Chapter 7. This chapter presents the three other defining parameters of a theme study: concept statements, guiding questions, and content summary.

Identifying the Concepts of a Theme

Once your team has identified a central focus for a theme study, it will select the broad concepts and generalizations that help define the scope of the study. To identify these concepts and essential understandings, the team must address the following central questions: What are the universal ideas in this theme study that will help students understand their world better? What lasting knowledge in this theme study is worth having? What knowledge in this theme study is most transferable?

When used in relation to curriculum, the term *concept* is defined as an organizing idea or broad category for thinking about a theme focus. Concepts represent a class of examples sharing common attributes. Some concepts are quite abstract, such as "conflict" or "system." Others, such as "color" or "family," are more concrete. Nevertheless, the concepts a team chooses for inclusion help to define the scope of a unit

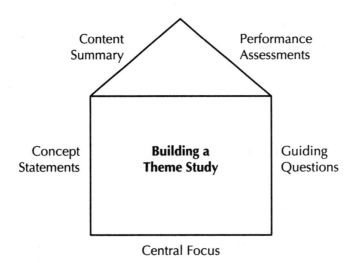

Figure 6.1   *Parameters of a Theme Study*

of instruction. Statements describing the relationships among major concepts or generalizations about important concepts are called "concept statements" or "essential understandings." Concept statements keep the curriculum focus on the most essential and universal aspects of the theme.

CHARACTERISTICS OF CONCEPT STATEMENTS   The five major characteristics exhibited by effective concept statements are illustrated in Figure 6.2.

Concept statements should make important generalizations. For guiding the curriculum, concept lists or captions using concepts are much less helpful than statements written to show generalizations or relationships among concepts. For example, a "desert" theme focus might include such concepts as desert animals, survival, and natural selection. A list of these concepts or even the caption "survival of desert animals" fails to help curriculum builders communicate the essential understandings worth pursuing in the theme study. However, a complete declarative statement like "The animal species living in the desert survive by natural selection" shows the important relationships among these concepts and communicates an essential understanding. For example, in a literature-based theme unit focusing on the book *Frederick*, the concepts of "the community" and "the arts" would be important. These concepts are put into relationship in the following concept statement: "Those who nurture the arts make a unique and valuable contribution to the community."

Concept statements should be broad. Concept statements represent major understandings that learners must construct for themselves by manipulating ideas and materials and interacting with a variety of resources and people. Concept statements go beyond facts and information. For example, one universal understanding is that animals in any environment are part of a food chain. Therefore, a team writing a resource unit with a focus of desert animals might choose to include this concept statement: "Desert animals are part of a food chain." Such

Figure 6.2 *Major Characteristics of Concept Statements*

> 1. Concept statements should make important generalizations.
> 2. Concept statements should be broad.
> 3. Concept statements should focus on content and not methodology.
> 4. Concept statements should help define the scope of the theme.
> 5. Concept statements should be developmentally appropriate.

a broad understanding suggests many investigations, projects, and experiences enabling students to understand this big idea. On the other hand, "The Kit Fox is a nocturnal hunter of small animals" offers factual information requiring no further investigation and thus would not be a concept statement. Such facts are meaningful only if students come to comprehend the broader understandings that they exemplify.

Concept statements should focus on the content to be learned, not the methodology. When formulating concept statements, ask yourself the question: "What essential understandings resulting from this theme study will be transferred and developed more fully three years from now?" A concept statement, however, does not address the ways that students arrive at these essential understandings. For example, it would not be appropriate to write as a concept statement: "Each student will complete an independent study of one desert animal." Such a statement reflects the means of achieving understanding rather than defining the desired understanding.

Concept statements, though few in number, should help define the scope of the unit. The concept statements that the team writes are not meant to include all of the learning taking place throughout the theme study. Indeed, because holistic experiences are gained throughout the unit, teachers may not anticipate many important understandings gained by the students. Many surprises and unintentional insights will delight both teacher and students. Also, specific objectives identified by the implementing teachers and learners during a theme study in one class may not be a priority for another class using the same theme resource unit. Students will often acquire interests during the theme study that concept statements do not address. However, the concept statements written by the team should be viewed as a few indispensable understandings providing valuable boundaries to give the study meaning, relevance, and depth. Most curriculum teams we have worked with have found that four to seven global understandings seem to define well the scope of their units.

Concept statements should be developmentally appropriate. Clearly, some concepts are more abstract than others and may be difficult for young children to construct. In addition, some concepts may not be adequately developed in the materials available at the students' reading levels and thus limit independent research. Therefore, teams may decide to postpone addressing some important concepts until later grades. Because they can be developed differently for different ages, many concepts will be revisited with a more complex treatment as students progress.

RECOMMENDED PROCESS FOR DEVELOPING CONCEPT STATEMENTS
Concept statements can be frustrating to write. However, because concept statements provide an essential part of the framework for your entire theme study, the time spent articulating, refining, and clarifying them is critical. Concept statements are derived in several ways. The first way is reflecting on what you know about your focus that is broadly transferable. A second way is researching the focus with an eye for the biggest ideas. The third way is brainstorming connecting concepts.

Charting What You Know and Want To Know. Your curriculum team may want to begin planning a theme study by reflecting on your current knowledge of the theme focus. For teams having a rich knowledge background of the theme focus, this approach works especially well. Chart what you know first and then add to this information any questions you would like to investigate. Organize what you know and want to know into categories using Action Pack 6-1 and the procedures below:

1. Working independently, record what you know or want to know about the chosen theme focus. Write each piece of information on a separate piece of paper.
2. As a team, organize all ideas into groups or categories sharing common characteristics.
3. Label each group with an organizing idea. Then transfer the labels to a beginning concept web.
4. Reorganize your idea cards from each group. Look for primary ideas and minor details. Document on the web the primary ideas offering supporting information under each of your major groups.

Figure 6.3 is a sample completed concept web for a theme on national parks.

Sometimes your team knows so little about the theme focus that you generate an insufficient number of facts or ideas to cluster. In this case, you must research fact sheets about the theme focus before doing the clustering activity.

> DOROTHY: *Working with a theme focus on ducks, a group of preservice teachers could write only a short list of facts they knew about ducks. The brevity of their list precluded finding concepts by clustering. I advised the team members to research ducks, preparing fact sheets. They came to a team meeting with strips of paper containing one fact each. The team was able to successfully cluster those facts into conceptually related groups. Using these groups, they identified some major concepts giving their theme study cohesiveness and substance.*

Carefully consider the major ideas on your web. They reflect what you currently think are the most significant ideas regarding this theme

Figure 6.3   *Sample Concept Web around Theme Focus of National Parks*

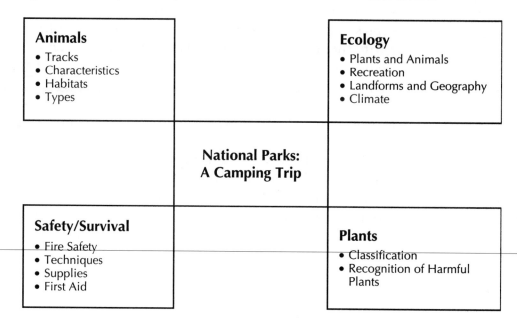

Animals
- Tracks
- Characteristics
- Habitats
- Types

Ecology
- Plants and Animals
- Recreation
- Landforms and Geography
- Climate

**National Parks:
A Camping Trip**

Safety/Survival
- Fire Safety
- Techniques
- Supplies
- First Aid

Plants
- Classification
- Recognition of Harmful Plants

focus, representing areas for which you might generate a concept statement. As you evaluate the ideas generated by this process for potential concept statements, ask yourselves how meaningful and relevant each of these concepts is for learners. For example, a team choosing a transportation focus might have these web headings: types, history, safety, and uses. This team must ask these questions: How important is it for students to understand types of transportation, history, safety issues, and uses? What aspects of these big ideas would be important for students of this age to understand? After reflecting on the uses of transportation, the team might write one concept statement as: "Transportation plays a vital role in meeting the needs of the people in a community."

Researching the Focus Looking for Big Ideas. Another technique for selecting meaningful concepts is to research your theme focus to find the most significant ideas presented in the available literature. When beginning research of a focus that is not literature based, start with nonfiction literature and information sources such as encyclopedias, textbooks, and the Internet. Content outlines and tables of contents are often helpful. As you survey these sources, ask yourself what subject-area experts seem to think are the most important and appropriate big ideas for students to understand. Use Action Pack 6-2 to guide your research.

Developing Concepts by Brainstorming. Brainstorming is usually profitable, sometimes even necessary, to identify concepts. In literature-based themes, the selected piece of literature is the hub for brainstorming major related issues, ideas, or critical connections that will represent the scope of the study. The key question to address in this brainstorming activity is this: What big issues or universal ideas connect to this piece of literature in a meaningful way? For example, a theme study based on *Frederick*, by Leo Lionni, might suggest exploring the issues of "interdependence," "creativity," "acceptance of differences," and "appreciation of the arts." Likewise "nature" or "a balanced life" might be identified as concepts worth exploring. Some teachers might value concepts about "the changing seasons," or "poetry as an art form" in connection with this piece of children's literature. Brainstorming possible related connections is also profitable for theme choices based on such abstract concepts as "survival" or "differences." Use Action Pack 6-3 when brainstorming concepts.

Team members need to compare the concepts or organizing ideas generated from three optional activities: charting what you know, researching, and brainstorming. Then the team must make some value judgments to answer the question: What knowledge is most valuable for our students? Once the team has agreed on the major concepts that members perceive to be most important, then it is ready to work on writing concept statements or essential understandings as clearly as possible. Record your chosen concept statements on Action Pack 6-4. Figures 6.4 through 6.7 provide examples of concept statements for the themes *Titanic*, Pittsburgh, whales, and fairy tales.

Crafting Guiding Questions

Most interdisciplinary thematic teaching approaches rely extensively on inductive reasoning to help students arrive at more general understandings. These approaches involve learners in gradually constructing broad understandings as they engage in numerous activities. Therefore, directly presenting the concept statements to students as advance organizers at the beginning of a theme study is not appropriate. However, students benefit greatly from having some guiding organizer from the

Figure 6.4 *Sample Concept Statements*

Concept Statements for a Theme Study on the *Titanic*

1. The *Titanic* sank because of a combination of extenuating circumstances and deliberate decisions.
2. Divisions between social classes had a large impact on the fate of those on the *Titanic*.
3. Moral issues surround both the sinking and resurrection of the *Titanic*.

Figure 6.5 *Sample Concept Statements*

Concept Statements for a Theme Study on Pittsburgh

1. The history of Pittsburgh influences its present and future.
2. The culture of Pittsburgh is colored by the diversity of its people.
3. The sports of Pittsburgh are important to its people and history.
4. The geography of Pittsburgh influences the various ways people and industrial materials are transported.
5. The industries of Pittsburgh rely on local natural resources.

---

outset of the theme study. One possibility is giving a few broad, interesting, and genuinely perplexing questions to the students. Unlike concept statements, which provide direction mainly for teachers, guiding questions are written for students. While numerous questions can be crafted to promote deep understanding throughout a theme study, "guiding questions" are the one or two questions used as a recurring focal point. Guiding questions should be broader than concept statements. Each question should be crafted as an invitation to students to wonder, search, and think.

Writing engaging, effective guiding questions will take practice. Indeed, part of a teacher's ongoing life work is the search for excellent questions that lead learners to construct understanding.

CHARACTERISTICS OF GUIDING QUESTIONS The work of Jacobs (1989, 1997) and Traver (1998) provide several suggestions for the criteria for good guiding questions. The following criteria will especially help

Figure 6.6 *Sample Concept Statements*

Concept Statements for a Theme Study on Variation among Whales

1. There are many kinds of whales in the oceans, but each kind has unique characteristics.
2. Whales can be found in a variety of habitats.
3. There is great variation in the reproductive habits of whales and in the care of their offspring.
4. Society needs to find strategies to address the endangerment of whales.

Figure 6.7   *Sample Concept Statements*

> ## Concept Statements for a Theme Study on Fairy Tales
>
> 1. The setting of a fairy tale is significant to the development of the story.
> 2. Fairy tales demonstrate the diversity that cultural influences bring to similar plots.
> 3. Fairy tales examine a wide variety of family structures.
> 4. Fairy tales contain unique characters who contribute to the theme of the story.

teams attempting to write guiding questions for their first theme studies. Figure 6.8 summarizes the recommendations for guiding questions.

Guiding questions should be broad and few in number. When they are broad, guiding questions give direction to student investigations without limiting creativity and interests. A theme study can be focused through just one or two "umbrella" guiding questions. If your team generates a much longer list, several questions could probably be categorized under others. To test whether the questions are broad enough, ask: Would each question require many activities to answer it? Do the questions connect to several disciplines? Is each question open-ended enough to invite speculation and hypothesizing? Do the questions allow for many points of view? Would students need to investigate more than one essential understanding to answer the guiding question? Are the questions nonrepetitive? Do the questions require students to compare information from several sources?

Guiding questions should point learners toward the priorities of the theme study. Answering the guiding questions should enable students to construct an understanding of the identified concept statements. Ask yourselves: Do these questions lead to an exploration of the concepts?

Figure 6.8   *Recommendations for Guiding Questions*

> 1. Use only one or two broad questions.
> 2. Use questions leading to the essential understandings.
> 3. Formulate questions in a way that motivates students.
> 4. Word questions so that students can easily understand them.
> 5. Refer to the questions frequently throughout the theme study.

DOROTHY: *A team of preservice teachers wrote this guiding question for their theme study on the city of Pittsburgh: "As a class, how are we like the city of Pittsburgh?" However, when they began to design performance assessments and activities, they found it very difficult to find projects embracing both their chosen concept statements and their guiding question. It seemed that their concepts suggested one set of activities and projects and their guiding question quite different activities. Clearly their guiding question was not working for them because it did not point to the priorities of the theme study. They formulated another question to focus students much more directly on the concepts of their theme: "How have its history and geography made Pittsburgh what it is today?"*

Guiding questions should be motivating. Work on the wording of the guiding questions until they are as intriguing as possible. Consider the motivational quality of these two guiding questions for a theme on the *Titanic:* "What would be done differently today than was done in 1912?" and "Why is there still a fascination with the *Titanic*?" Guiding questions should be viewed as compelling invitations to students to find out, think for themselves, and make judgments. The best questions also create in learners a disposition to pose additional questions.

Guiding questions should be easy for students to understand. They should be succinct and simply worded. Simple questions can be powerful ones. Often guiding questions make use of these key words: who, what, where, when, how, and why. "How can you help the whales?" is simple, direct, and yet compelling. Sometimes, in order to invite speculation, the word "true" or "good" or "best" is used, as in "Who is a true hero?" or "What is a good diet?" or "Which is the best fairy tale?"

To maximize their impact, guiding questions should be prominently displayed in the classroom and referred to often. Teachers should rely on the questions as they decide which activities and experiences to pursue and which to bypass. As teachers and students use concept statements and guiding questions to direct their activity choices, they find themselves going a long way toward creating a cohesive and purposeful theme study.

LINDA: *When I developed my Theme Box on the African grasslands, my team and I had not heard of guiding questions. During my student teaching experience, I had the opportunity to create and implement an integrated teaching unit using my Theme Box. As my cooperating teacher and I discussed possible assessments for the unit completion, we decided that the second grade students should draw conclusions about the differences and similarities of their lives and a child's life in the African grasslands. As the unit continued, I found myself asking the children these two questions at the conclusion of each activity: "How is life in Charleroi, Pennsylvania, different from life in the African grasslands?" and "How is life in Charleroi, Pennsylvania, similar to life in the African grasslands?" The students began to search for similarities and differences in the activities they initiated. In reflecting on my unit, I began to see that those questions had guided my facilitation of activities and direct teaching. In fact, I now wish that in our daily journals we had documented the answers we found as a class. I didn't realize it at the time, but I had found not only the guiding questions for my particular theme study but also the value and use of guiding questions generally.*

Use Action Pack 6-5 to generate possible guiding questions for your theme.

Summarizing the Content

To achieve clarity on the content to be included in a theme study, summarizing and organizing the topics for study is important. We present three effective alternative devices for summarizing the most important content of a theme study: content webs, background information reports, and content questions.

CONTENT WEBS A content web is effective in showing at a glance the interrelationships of the content. It brings into focus the most important understandings. This type of organizer assists teachers implementing theme studies when making decisions about selecting objectives, organizing time, sequencing experiences, and choosing activities. Webs can organize content in three different formats. First, a team might use the broadest concepts as the major categories of the web subsuming supporting facts and information. Such is the case in Figure 6.9, a sample content web for a theme on whales. Second, teams may prefer an organizational scheme where examples are the major categories and concepts are subsumed under them. Such is the case in Figure 6.10, a sample content web for a theme on fairy tales. A third type of content web format organizes the content around disciplines connected to the theme study. For example, this type of content web might include the science content, the social studies content, and the fine art content to be integrated into a theme on heroes. Teams composed of members from specialized disciplines may prefer this discipline-based web type since each specialist can see exactly what content will be included from his discipline. Figure 6.11 provides an example of a discipline-based content organizer for a theme on American Heroines. This web summarizes content from *Focus on Women* (Davis & Selvidge, 1995). Use Action Pack 6-6 to create a content web for your focus.

Figure 6.9   *Sample Web with Concepts as Major Points for a Theme on Whales*

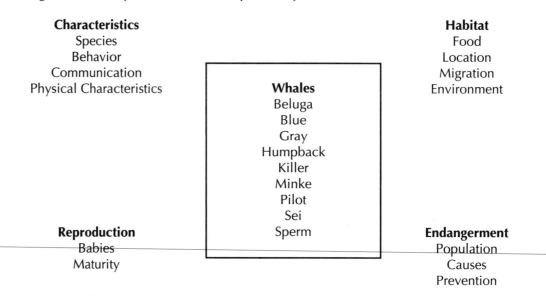

BACKGROUND REPORTS   Many teams opt to go beyond a content web by writing background reports on their research. These reports serve two purposes: first, they are a service to the classroom teachers implementing the theme study; and second, they are a way for the curriculum writing team to become more informed on the focus. Since the intended audience for these background reports is teachers, not students, some information will not be developed with students.

Figure 6.10   *Sample Web with Concepts as Supporting Points*

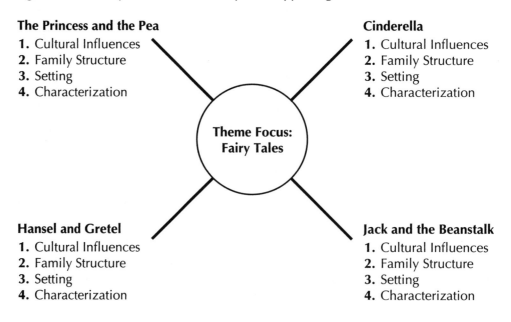

Figure 6.11   *Sample Web Organized around Disciplines for a Theme on American Heroines*

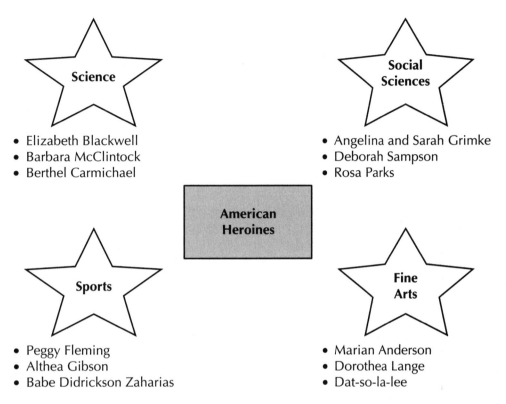

Science

- Elizabeth Blackwell
- Barbara McClintock
- Berthel Carmichael

Social Sciences

- Angelina and Sarah Grimke
- Deborah Sampson
- Rosa Parks

American Heroines

Sports

- Peggy Fleming
- Althea Gibson
- Babe Didrickson Zaharias

Fine Arts

- Marian Anderson
- Dorothea Lange
- Dat-so-la-lee

Dividing the work for writing background reports works well. Using a "jigsaw approach," each team member might become an expert on one or more of the concepts or content sections. In addition to traditional library or periodical research, the Internet has opened up many new ways to find background information. Web sites of museums, national societies, television stations, and library home pages provide excellent current information. Many encyclopedias are now available on CD-ROM or via a web interface. Some encyclopedia programs are interactive and will search the Internet on your topic. If you are unfamiliar with the Internet, your school or community library media specialist is a good resource person to guide you.

Figure 6.12 provides one theme builder's account of successfully using the Internet for researching background information for a theme study on whales. As a teacher conducts a web search on a theme focus, she can simultaneously be checking the links for content and age appropriateness for later student use.

To prepare a well-designed theme resource book, teams should agree on some criteria for the information reports. Figure 6.13 provides a sample rubric for evaluating a background information report. While the sample rubric provides quality indicators, it does not address the issues of style, approximate length, number of sources, and format of

Figure 6.12   *A Narrative on Internet Use for a Theme Study on Whales*

To access various web sites, I first went to Yahoo, a general search engine. From Yahoo, I typed in the broad topic of whales. When I looked through the connections, I found over 100,000 connections to web sites on whales. Then I began a new search by typing in a specific whale, which narrowed the web site connections significantly.

I scanned through the connections to see what web sites would be most likely to have reliable information. I looked for sites sponsored by whale organizations such as Save the Whales International, large metropolitan zoos, or educational organizations. I had the e-mail address for Sea World/Busch Gardens, so I e-mailed them for information. They sent back the web address to their educational site on the Internet. I also had the *Free Willy* videos, which gave the web site address for the Free Willy Keiko Foundation. I pulled up the information from this site.

Then I started to think about television stations and magazines with web sites containing valuable information. I found web addresses by watching the Discovery Channel, the History Channel, and CNN News. I found the site for National Geographic.

In time, by "surfing the net," I compiled an entire resource collection, providing information from many reputable organizations. Later, when looking for theme activities, I accessed the ERIC Digest, listed whales as my topic, and found numerous journal articles and books with activities and ideas. I also went through Internet sources and indexes on the library home page to find activities. Sea World and Enchanted Learning Software had numerous activities on their web sites. A large number of teacher web sites have valuable activities and ideas already proven successful in the classroom.

presentation. Action Pack 6-7 will help you develop your own rubric to clarify these issues.

Each author should evaluate her own report using the rubrics. Then peers may edit one another's reports using the rubrics. Peer editing within a group enables authors to have the best advice from other group members. Also, the entire team becomes fully informed on the topics and maintains awareness of the total resource book development. Peer editors are advised to make summary comments on an evaluation sheet and also mark places where the draft needs corrections. Another function the peer editor performs is leading the team in discussing significant questions requiring additional research. Generally, all group members serve as peer editors. A sample peer editor's response form is provided in Action Pack 6-8. As group members share their progress, the team often decides to change the agreed-upon criteria or rubrics.

Figure 6.13 *Sample Rubric of Quality Indicators for Background Reports*

Exceptional

1. Sharp, distinct focus
2. Substantial, specific, and/or illustrative content
3. Sophisticated, well-developed ideas
4. Logical order and sequence
5. Strong presence of writer's voice
6. Few mechanical and usage errors
7. Appropriate information for the audience and task
8. Effective introduction and conclusion
9. Outstanding reader appeal
10. Effective use of resources and citations

Acceptable

1. Adequate focus
2. Sufficient content
3. Well-developed major points
4. Appropriate organization
5. Some precision and variety in sentence structure and word choice
6. Minor mechanical and usage errors
7. Awareness of audience and task
8. Adequate introduction and conclusion
9. Adequate reader appeal
10. Appropriate use of resources and citations

Not Acceptable

1. Confused focus
2. Superficial content
3. Naive, obvious ideas
4. Confused organization
5. Unvaried sentence and word choice
6. Severe mechanical and usage errors
7. Inappropriate content for audience or task
8. Unclear and ineffective introduction and conclusion
9. Insufficient reader appeal
10. Inadequate use of resources and citations

Therefore, original agreements should be viewed as tentative until further progress is made on the work. Generally, the author or appointed project editor has the final say on a report and does the final revising and editing. The team should agree on the amount of time allowed for peer editing and final revisions.

Once teams have completed background research reports, they should schedule meeting time to share the information. Each team member will then present what he has learned to the team. This is a good time to re-examine concept statements and guiding questions. Guided by more substantial background knowledge, the team can determine if they still reflect the desired parameters for the theme study.

CONTENT QUESTIONS Teams with thorough knowledge of their theme focus may choose an alternative to background reports by developing a series of questions for students. These questions should reflect the essence of the content. Carefully constructed content questions are powerful in guiding students. In concert with the overall guiding questions, content questions reflect the most important issues for students to explore.

Content questions should be written at various levels. Certainly, some important questions will be at a basic knowledge or comprehension level. But most questions should promote critical thinking by requiring learners to apply, analyze, synthesize, hypothesize, and evaluate. Using Bloom's taxonomy of objectives (1956) to develop a question set for each concept statement is a workable approach to writing effective questions that summarize the content. In this way, you ensure that your content questions address all the theme study priorities. Action Pack 6-9 provides a guide for question writing.

Reporting the Parameters of a Theme Study

Once the team develops parameters defining a theme study, it should summarize them on a single piece of paper. This theme study overview enables the team to have a ready reference when making important decisions about activities and supplemental resources to be included in the Theme Box. Figure 6.14 provides a one-page overview example for a theme study on natural disasters. Action Pack 6-10 provides a planning form for your team to use when recording the parameters of your theme study.

CONCLUSION

The parameters defining the structure of a theme study are as follows: (1) the central focus, (2) the concept statements, (3) the guiding questions, (4) the content summary, and (5) the performance assessments addressing the concept statements and guiding questions. Once these aspects are in place, the team has built a structure for a coherent, pur-

Figure 6.14   *Sample Theme Study Overview*

Theme Focus: Natural Disasters   **Grade Level:** Upper Elementary

Guiding Questions

If you had to choose among living near an earthquake fault line, a dry forest, a riverbank, or near tropical waters that produce hurricanes, where would you live and why?

Concept Statements

1. Natural disasters have devastating economic consequences.

2. Natural disasters are unique to specific geographic regions.

3. Technology has enabled us to minimize the effects of natural disasters through advance warnings that allow time to prepare.

4. Natural disasters take a large emotional toll on the nation.

Performance Assessments

Assessment #1: Students will create a news broadcast and commercials. This newscast will include descriptions of natural disasters taking place around the world. Students will warn the viewers of impending disasters and offer safety tips to help them prepare for and survive the storm, flood, fire, or earthquake. Students will also explain the science behind the disaster. The commercial breaks will be created to persuade viewers to move to certain areas of the country. The commercials will include positive aspects of each area and comparisons with other trouble spots.

Assessment #2: Students will create a "Disaster Handbook." This handbook will provide valuable information on how to best survive a natural disaster and precautions or preventative measures that should be observed when encountering a disaster. A list of first aid and emergency materials needed and a list of resource agencies and community shelters to contact for extra help will also be included in the handbook.

Content Summary

Fire	Earthquake
1. Geographic Regions	1. Geographic Regions
2. Economic Consequences	2. Economic Consequences
3. Emotional Consequences	3. Emotional Consequences
4. Technology	4. Technology

Natural Disasters

Hurricanes	Floods
1. Geographic Regions	1. Geographic Regions
2. Economic Consequences	2. Economic Consequences
3. Emotional Consequences	3. Emotional Consequences
4. Technology	4. Technology

poseful study that can lead students to meaningful knowledge. In order to be effective, concept statements and guiding questions must have certain important characteristics. Teams need to write and evaluate concept statements and guiding questions with these in mind. Teams can summarize the content of a theme study through content webs, background reports, and content questions. Carefully considering the most important content will help to guarantee that your theme study has genuine substance.

Chapter 7 offers an in-depth discussion of the last essential parameter of a theme study: performance assessments. Other aspects of assessment are also introduced because of their value in making student learning visible.

Instructions

1. Using 3×5 cards or "post it" notes, individually record what "you know" or "want to know." Each card or note should contain only one idea.
2. As a team, organize your idea cards into groups or categories that share common characteristics.
3. Using either a word or phrase, create a label for each group. Transfer these labels to the concept web below or create your own web to better fit your information.
4. Reorganize your idea cards from each group. Look for primary ideas and minor details. On the web, represent the primary ideas as supporting information below your major group labels.

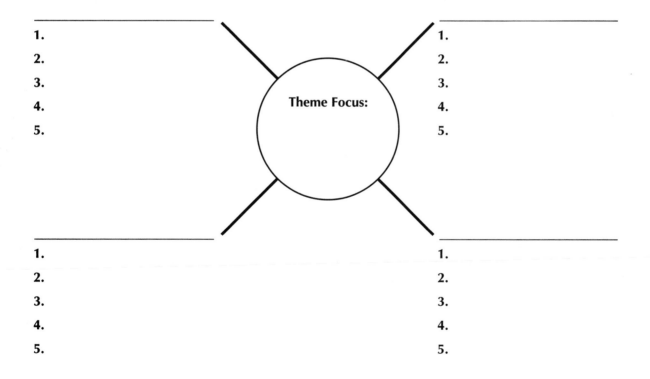

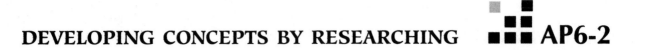
Encyclopedia: Look up your focus topic in an encyclopedia. Consider using an encyclopedia on CD-ROM or an index from a library home page. Look for the major categories or divisions. What major questions are answered?

Name of Encyclopedia (include all bibliographical data):

Main Ideas:

Internet: Search the Internet for two or three web sites on your focus topic.

Web Site Addresses:

Main Ideas:

Theme-Related Literature: Survey a piece of age-appropriate nonfiction literature. Look at the table of contents and major headings. What major ideas are addressed?

Book Title (include all bibliographical data):

Main Ideas:

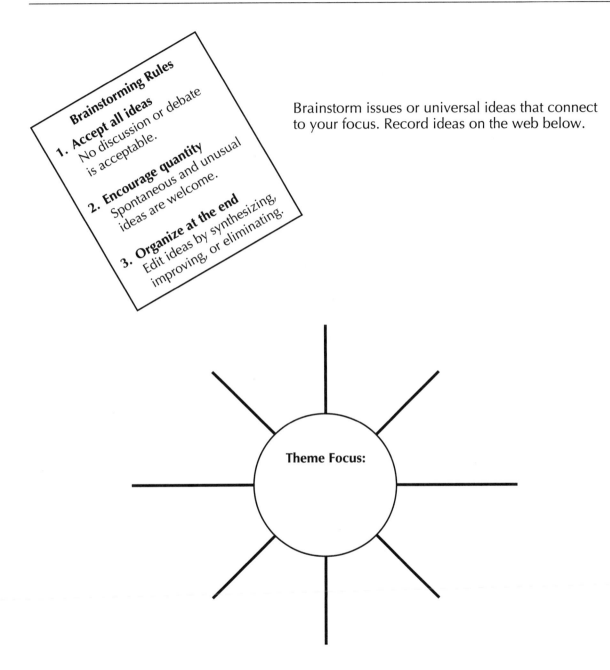

Brainstorming Rules

1. Accept all ideas
No discussion or debate is acceptable.

2. Encourage quantity
Spontaneous and unusual ideas are welcome.

3. Organize at the end
Edit ideas by synthesizing, improving, or eliminating.

Brainstorm issues or universal ideas that connect to your focus. Record ideas on the web below.

Theme Focus:

Compare the concept ideas from Action Packs 6-1 to 6-3. Arrive at team consensus on the most valuable knowledge for students. Choose the concepts that will guide your theme study. List them below:

Concepts

1.

2.

3.

4.

5.

Using the following criteria, rewrite final concept statements.

    a. Concepts should be broad.
    b. Concepts should be written as complete declarative sentences.
    c. Concepts should focus on content, not methodology.
    d. Concepts should define the scope of the theme.
    e. Concepts should be developmentally appropriate.

Final Concept Statements

1.

2.

3.

4.

5.

To ensure that your guiding questions point learners toward the priorities of the theme study, list your chosen concept statements below:

Looking at your concept statements, brainstorm "who," "what," "where," "when," "how," and "why" questions that address more than one and preferably several of your concepts.

Cluster similar questions and eliminate repetition. Use these groups to write one to three broad "umbrella" guiding questions. Remember that they should motivate learners, communicate clearly to students, and focus learning around the concepts.

1.

2.

3.

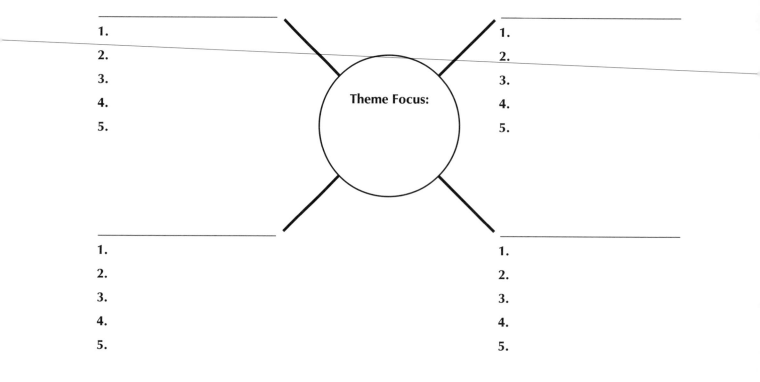

_____
1.
2.
3.
4.
5.

Theme Focus:

_____
1.
2.
3.
4.
5.

_____
1.
2.
3.
4.
5.

_____
1.
2.
3.
4.
5.

Use the categories below, plus any others that your team values, to design your own rubric for style and quantity indicators for information reports.

Style and Quantity Indicators

Exceptional

1. Length

2. Number of sources

3. Number of main points

4. Style

5. Format

Acceptable

1. Length

2. Number of sources

3. Number of main points

4. Style

5. Format

Not Acceptable

1. Length

2. Number of sources

3. Number of main points

4. Style

5. Format

PEER EDITOR REACTION SHEET

 AP6-8

Author's Name: _____

Editor's Name: _____

Perceived Strengths (+)

_____

_____

_____

_____

_____

_____

Apparent Weaknesses (–)

_____

_____

_____

_____

_____

_____

Tentative Suggestions (?)

_____

_____

_____

_____

_____

_____

Overall rating on this draft:

_____ Professional paper—ready for publication

_____ Draft—still needs some work

Using Bloom's (1956) cognitive domain taxonomy as a guide, write questions of varying levels to summarize content for each of your concept statements.

Level 1—Knowledge: recalling specific information
Level 2—Comprehension: recognizing or restating information in a different form
Level 3—Application: performing actions with information
Level 4—Analysis: breaking down information and clarifying the relationships
                              between parts
Level 5—Synthesis: creating something unique by using information in a new way
Level 6—Evaluation: using information to make a judgment of worth

Concept Statement No. _____

Questions:

Note: Make a duplicate of this page for each concept statement.

Theme Focus: _____ **Grade Level:** _____

Guiding Questions	Performance Assessments
Concept Statements	
	Content Summary

CHAPTER 7

Making Learning Visible through Varied Assessment

GUIDING QUESTIONS

What Is the Value of Varied Assessment?
How Can Student Learning Be Made Visible?
How Can the School Curriculum Be Made Visible?

The purpose of assessment in thematic instruction is to make learning visible so that schools, teachers, and students can demonstrate student attainment of deep understanding. Two important approaches make visible the learning achieved through integrated theme studies. The first is a direct assessment of the knowledge constructed by students about selected themes in individual classes. When assessing students' gains, teachers always need to emphasize what was learned rather than what was taught. When teaching is stressed, teachers tend to measure success by listing the content and skills "covered." However, when learning is emphasized, teachers base success on the extent of student understanding and competencies, or what was "uncovered." The second approach to making learning visible is aimed at assessment of the overall school program related to theme studies. The total school curriculum is assessed in terms of balance, coverage, and appropriateness.

WHAT IS THE VALUE OF VARIED ASSESSMENT?

Learners can show what they know in a number of ways. Sometimes they best communicate their understandings orally; other times they communicate best through writing. At times, students construct models to show what they have learned. If a teacher wants the fullest understanding of what individual learners know, she needs to use a wide range of assessment strategies. If data is gathered about student learning through a variety of techniques, a much more detailed picture of individual students emerges. Then more appropriate objectives can be set, more effective instructional strategies can be used, and ultimately it can be determined if goals have been met. Moreover, as students review the documentation of their own learning, they have a better understanding of where they have been and where they are going. From this knowledge, students gradually learn to evaluate their own progress and set goals for their own learning. As students see visible signs of their development, they gain a sense of pride and ownership in their learning.

A rich documentation of student learning has other benefits as well. It facilitates communication with parents about their children's development and progress. Seeing a full documentation of learning rather than merely a report card with letter grades, parents gain important insights into their children's progress and achievements. Multiple assessment strategies yield information that is specific and complete enough to enable both teachers and parents to formulate ways to assist in building on strengths and improving weaknesses.

HOW CAN STUDENT LEARNING BE MADE VISIBLE?

Student learning should be made visible in many ways. Students are assessed more fairly and more fully when teachers use a variety of strategies rather than over-relying on tests. In this chapter we will discuss five major methods of assessing student learning: performance assessments, teacher observations, processfolios and process journals, portfolios, and self-evaluation. Each of these broad categories encompasses many options for obtaining data beyond standardized and teacher-constructed tests. Of all the options presented in this chapter, performance assessment receives the most attention because it is the type best generated by the curriculum team.

Performance Assessments

A performance assessment is a project or task that is broad in scope, addressing many, if not all, of the chosen concepts and guiding questions. Performance assessments enable students to synthesize learning occurring throughout the theme study to create something new: a product or a performance. Performance assessments provide opportunities for students to show what they have learned in creative ways rather than through answering specific questions. Requiring divergent thinking, performance assessments include such projects as producing news broadcasts, plays, or writing projects. Performance assessments typically require a wide repertoire of skills. To achieve excellence, students are required to revise the performance or product. Furthermore, to enhance relevance, teachers devise performance assessments that are authentic. They design ways for students to show understanding in a manner similar to people's use of that knowledge in the real world. Figure 7.1 is an example of a performance assessment description requiring students to combine the information gathered from research on several aspects of National Parks with many writing and artistic skills to design a brochure and a commercial to advertise a National Park.

Performance assessments are most effectively designed by teams rather than by individual teachers. Teams of teachers can use their creative synergy and collective judgment while designing this form of assessment. If the curriculum team creating a theme study generates at least two performance assessments, implementing teachers have some options.

Figure 7.1   *Sample Performance Assessment for a Theme on National Parks*

Theme Focus: Our National Parks: A Camping Trip

Guiding Question: What makes this park extraordinary?

Performance Assessment:

Students will work in small groups to create brochures and commercials for chosen National Parks. In addition to addressing the concepts about the National Parks, this activity would also use a variety of skills in many areas. Each brochure must include these seven aspects about the park: location, plants and animals that live there, the geography, the climate, camping safety, its value to the nation, and the protection of the park. The students will also draw at least four pictures representing the park's uniqueness and illustrating the beauty and significance of the park. In addition, each group will draw a map, complete with a key and written directions for getting from their school to the park. Exactness is not the primary purpose of these maps; the aim is for the children to understand their function and purpose. Students will peer edit each other's written work before writing the final copy. Once the brochures are completed, students will make commercials for their parks. The students must highlight unique qualities of each park. If a group has created a song, it can be incorporated into their commercial. Videotaping the commercials adds to the importance of the project, and also can serve as a means of self-reflection for the students.

A performance assessment project or task is an excellent place to integrate important skills into a theme study. Essential skills articulated in state and district guidelines should be assigned a definite place in the curriculum. When embedded in performance assessments, the skills are taught within a meaningful context rather than in isolation. Complex skills are applied and evident in the final product or performance. Therefore, curriculum committees must consciously determine which critical thinking skills, social skills, literacy skills, and mathematical skills can be effectively addressed in each performance assessment. Figure 7.2 provides a list of skills addressed through a performance assessment for the theme *Titanic.* The assessment project

Figure 7.2   *Sample Skill Objectives for a Theme Study on the* Titanic

Theme Focus: *Titanic*

Guiding Questions:

What could we do differently today than was done in 1912?

Why is there still so much fascination with the *Titanic* today?

Performance Assessment:

A debate on issues surrounding the *Titanic*

Skills:

1. The students will speak with an awareness of audience and task.

2. The students will establish and maintain a clear purpose.

3. The students will sustain a single point of view.

4. The students will communicate ideas clearly.

5. The students will use precise language.

6. The students will make effective word choices.

7. The students will exhibit originality of language.

8. The students will use information and details specific to the topic.

9. The students will manage available time well.

10. The students will listen to others speak and respond appropriately.

was a debate on issues surrounding the exploration and resurrection of the *Titanic.*

While some assessments of this type are short-term and limited in focus, many performance assessments are long-term projects taking over a great deal of the actual teaching plan for the theme study. For this reason, performance assessments should be formulated prior to developing the rest of the teaching unit plan. As the project progresses, teachers maximize opportunities to provide experiences to help learners construct understandings critical to successful completion of the project. Inevitably, students will require coaching on some of the skills required to complete the project. Both teachers and students emphasize the learning and synthesizing processes involved in creating a final product or performance.

Teams creating performance assessments will benefit from following a step-by-step procedure until experienced with this kind of assessment. The following guidelines suggest such a procedure. Action Packs 7-1 to 7-8 can assist teams in this procedure.

STEP ONE: BRAINSTORMING PERFORMANCE ASSESSMENT OPTIONS

Brainstorm a list of possible projects or tasks for assessing understanding of the chosen concepts. Make sure that brainstormed assessments require students to answer the guiding question(s). Some suggestions on your list might be rather narrow, while others might be broader. Figure 7.3 provides a sample of this step in the process for a theme on the African grasslands. Action Pack 7-1 will serve to guide teams in this step.

STEP TWO: CHOOSING PERFORMANCE ASSESSMENTS   Narrow your choices by using these evaluation questions:

1. Which choices best reflect what we really want our students to be able to do as a result of this theme study?
2. Which choices most directly focus on the guiding questions of the theme study?
3. Which choices would be impossible to do unless the concepts were well understood?
4. Which choices best require application, analysis, and synthesis of the theme content?
5. Which choices best reflect real-world applications of knowledge from this theme study?
6. Which choices require skills that are appropriate and valuable for our students?
7. Which choices are challenging yet developmentally appropriate?
8. Which choices are most worth the time and effort required to complete?

Figure 7.3 *Sample of Step One: Brainstorming Performance Assessments*

Theme Focus: African Grasslands

Concepts:

1. The climate of the African savanna plays a major role in the animal and plant life of the area. The lives of the people are also affected by the weather.
2. The wet and dry seasons have determined the varieties of grasses and trees growing in the African savanna.
3. A wide variety of animals, many unique to the African grasslands, roam freely on the savanna. Many of these species are endangered.
4. The African savanna is home to a vast diversity of peoples with rich and varied cultures.
5. The African savanna, a tropical grassland covering 40 percent of the continent of Africa, is one of many grasslands throughout the world.

Guiding Questions:

1. How is the life of a child in the African grasslands different from a child's life in Western Pennsylvania?
2. How is the life of a child in the African grasslands similar to a child's life in Western Pennsylvania?

Brainstormed Performance Assessments Addressing Concepts and Questions:

Keep a daily learning journal
Design a three-section mural (life in Pennsylvania; life in Africa; things we share)
Create an interactive Venn diagram (flannel board)
Write and produce a three-act play
Present a musical using ballads from Africa, Pennsylvania, and from the African American culture
Produce a TV news-journal show
Write a magazine with articles based on essential questions

Use Action Pack 7-2 to evaluate your options. Choose your two best ideas to develop into performance assessment projects. For each selected option, complete steps three to seven.

STEP THREE: DRAFTING PERFORMANCE ASSESSMENT DESCRIPTIONS
Write an outline for each performance assessment option selected including as much detailed information as you can. As you work through the remaining steps, you will no doubt change your task or project con-

ception. Your outline can be altered to reflect these changes. Use Action Pack 7-3 to document this step.

STEP FOUR: BRAINSTORMING ENRICHMENT POSSIBILITIES Brainstorm ways that each performance assessment option might allow students to use a number of the intelligences that Gardner (1993) defined. This activity will enable your team to see new possibilities for ways learners can show what they know. From the ideas brainstormed, choose those the team values for inclusion in your performance assessment. Action Pack 7-4 will guide this brainstorming phase. Figure 7.4 provides a sample of this step for a performance assessment for a theme study on the farm.

STEP FIVE: IDENTIFYING THE CONTENT GOALS Identify the content goals or general purposes for the performance assessment task. This is done by answering the following questions: What lasting knowledge do we want students to demonstrate through this performance assessment? How can they demonstrate that they have answered the guiding question(s)? Most of the content goals tie directly into the chosen concepts. Later in the implementation stage, teachers will identify the related specific, observable objectives most appropriate for their particular students. Use Action Pack 7-5 for planning this part of the performance assessment. Figure 7.5 provides a list of content goals for a performance assessment on fairy tales.

STEP SIX: IDENTIFYING PROCESS AND SKILL GOALS Identify the essential skills and processes that will be embedded into each performance assessment. When making this determination, your curriculum team should refer to your state standards and district requirements. Be sure to consider a full range of skills including critical thinking, social, literacy, and mathematical skills. Write these skills and processes as general purpose statements. Use Action Pack 7-6 as a guide.

STEP SEVEN: REVISING PERFORMANCE ASSESSMENTS Write the performance assessment paragraph description. Check that it includes ways to enrich the project by addressing the multiple intelligences. Revise and edit this performance assessment description and your list of goals and skills. You may wish to use Action Pack 7-7 to work out your final draft. Figure 7.6 provides a performance assessment description for a theme study on fairy tales.

STEP EIGHT: DESIGNING ACTIVITIES Using the performance assessment descriptions as guides, either the curriculum writing team or the implementing teachers will need to identify and describe all the activities inherent in the chosen performance assessment. For some performance

Figure 7.4   *Sample of a Multiple-Intelligence Brainstorm for a Theme on Farm Animals*

Theme Focus: Farm Animals

Performance Assessment: Chick Hatching/Embryology Project

Overall Goals:

The students will learn responsibility while caring for another living thing.
The students will develop a respect for life.
The students will recognize the main parts of a developing chick.
The students will recognize the parts of an egg.
The students will understand the developmental processes and growth stages of a chick.
The students will understand the concept of reproduction as it applies to chickens.

Activity Options:

Linguistic Intelligence
Writing news articles about the developing chick. Minilessons on news article research and formats should be taught if needed. The completed articles could be showcased on a bulletin board or in a school newspaper.

Writing imaginative stories. Give children a story starter such as, "One day in our classroom our chick eggs began to hatch, but instead out popped a _____." Or use an interesting title for which the students will write a story, such as "Monster Egg" or "The Mysterious Egg."

Logical Mathematical Intelligence
Making predictions. The children can hypothesize about these various aspects of the project: appearance of chicks when hatched, color of chicks, and hatching date and time of chicks. Chart their predictions in a class journal or bulletin board. Check throughout project to see if predictions are correct.

Charting activities. Chart the temperature and weight of the eggs daily. Compare to available published charts.

Bodily Kinesthetic Intelligence
Simulating movements. Have children pretend they are chicks inside the shell about to hatch. The students can curl up into the smallest possible position, inside a hula hoop or a large pillow case, and pretend to be chicks hatching out of the shell. Prior class discussion will help students understand the timing and importance of this process to the chick.

Figure 7.4 (continued)

Visual Spatial Intelligence

Creating sequential books. Have students create a sequential book showing the developmental stages of the chick within the egg. This could be done in one- or five-day increments. The illustrations can be hand-drawn or reproduced from another source and colored appropriately.

Creating photo albums. Have the class begin by taking photos to document all phases of preparation, incubator set up, taking weights and measurements, the actual hatching, and the baby chicks after they are born. Place these in an album and label appropriately. This photo album of the chick-hatching project can be shared with other classes or with students' families.

Musical Intelligence

Writing songs. Write, sing, and act out a farming song, sung to the tune of "Farmer in the Dell." Include verses for the hatching of chicks.

Interpersonal Intelligence

Group presenting. Each group of students will give a presentation on the chick hatching project. Groups will research and prepare presentations on these or other topics: Art We Have Made about Chicks, Parts of an Egg, Developmental Stages, Temperature/Measurement. Invite families or another class to view final presentations. (This idea would also be excellent for enhancing linguistic intelligence.)

Planning a party. Students send out "birth announcements" to prospective guests, plan refreshments related to theme, and celebrate the birth of the chicks. This could be done in conjunction with the presentations on the project.

Intrapersonal Intelligence

Setting goals. When discussing the hatching process of the chicks and perseverance necessary for a chick to emerge from its shell, have students decide on a personal goal to achieve. Record these goals and a plan of achievement in personal journals. Have students track and reflect on their progress toward achieving their goal.

Naturalist Intelligence

Charting Development. The class will construct a Chick Check Chart. As a class or individually construct a chart documenting changes, temperature, humidity, turning times, and other pertinent records. Regularly check the development of the chicks and record the findings on the chart.

Figure 7.5 *Sample Content Goals for a Theme on Fairy Tales*

Theme Focus: Fairy Tales

Guiding Question: Which element do you believe is most important to the development of this story and why?

Content Goals:

1. The students will gain an appreciation of other cultures.
2. The students will value fairy tales as a form of literature.
3. The students will empathize with different family structures.
4. The students will understand that characters contribute to the theme of a fairy tale.
5. The students will understand the significance of the setting to the development of the story.

---

assessments, there may be a single task resulting in a very specific, focused performance or product. However, most performance assessments will involve several classroom activities. Many of these activities will yield a product or performance that will be part of the final product or performance. For each activity, the teacher or team should generate a description that includes a list of materials, step-by-step procedures, possible adaptations and, where appropriate, the resulting product or performance. Action Pack 7-8 provides a format for documenting your activity ideas.

When actually implementing the performance assessment, teachers will need to identify standards of excellence for each product or performance resulting from these activities. Once a performance assessment has been tried with students generating actual work samples, teachers will inevitably make further criteria refinements. Then rubrics can be designed. Additionally, implementing teachers must make decisions about choices students will be given during the performance assessment project. These include choices about topics, products, partners, and optional activities. Implementing teachers must also determine the amount of time committed to the assessment, the amount of coaching required, the degree of help needed with identifying resources, and the profile of the audience for the product or performance.

Assessing through Observations

Teacher observation is an excellent way to learn about the specific needs and achievements of a group as well as individual students. When done frequently, systematically, and objectively, teacher observation provides data from which you can determine trends and dispositions.

Figure 7.6   *Sample Performance Assessment Description for a Theme on Fairy Tales*

Theme Focus: Fairy Tales

Guiding Question: Which element do you believe is most important to the development of this story and why?

Performance Assessment Description:

The teacher will prepare four cans with the following labels: cultures, settings, families, and characterizations. She will place in these cans strips of paper listing specific ideas that fit under each of the headings. Each student will choose one strip of paper from each can. The four elements chosen by the student will determine the basic structure for the fairy tale he will compose. For example, if a child chooses "Chinese," "stepfamily," "forest," and "princess," these will be the basic elements contained in his story.

In cooperative groups, the students will research all of the elements that they have selected. Because there will be more than one of each element in the cans, several students will have the same element. Each student will be placed into four groups, based on his designated culture, family, characterization, and setting elements. After gaining information on their elements, the students will begin writing their individual fairy tales incorporating information they have learned and using sequencing and creative writing skills.

After students complete the writing, they will self-evaluate and then peer edit the fairy tales. Each student will create a picture book with illustrations. At an authors' day, the students will share the books with their class and families. The class will decide which element had the greatest impact on each story.

From these trends and dispositions, you can plan a developmentally appropriate curriculum and evaluate success in achieving objectives.

The goal of all teacher observation is to seek a full understanding and to avoid premature judgments. Allowing yourself to embark on an observation with a prior judgment about a student's abilities will bias what you see and may obscure the truth. Often, first impressions persist. Therefore, teachers must consciously strive to maintain the professional discipline of objectivity.

DATA COLLECTION FORMS   Systematic forms of data collecting will help you meet the challenges of objectivity, accuracy, and confidentiality. Some examples of these techniques include time samples, event samples, checklists, rating scales, sociograms, frequency charts and anecdotal records.

Time samples require recording behavior at regular, predetermined intervals. For example, a teacher might observe and record what is happening in a particular cooperative learning group every five minutes, taking about three minutes to observe and two minutes to record objective notes. Trends and implications can then be identified.

Event samples focus on a specific phenomena or problem that is recurring on a regular basis. The purpose of event sampling is to explore the causes and effects of the behavior. This observation strategy is commonly used when a child or group is frequently engaging in an inappropriate or ineffective behavior or when a child is displaying atypical behavior.

Rating checklists and scales are sometimes used to make observations easier and less time consuming. With checklists, behaviors are usually identified as either present or absent. Rating scales allow a degree to be indicated. For example, many rating scales use the following degrees: never, seldom, sometimes, often, and always. Checklists and rating scales have the advantage of indicating precisely which behaviors are to be observed.

Sociograms focus on student interactions with peers. As teachers observe students interacting in groups, they can study preferences for peers as well as group dynamics. This data can be used for planning curriculum, promoting social development, and building heterogeneous cooperative learning groups.

Frequency charts are used to tally the instances of a particular behavior within an identified time frame. For example, a teacher might observe a small group discussion, tallying the number of times each student in the group offered information or asked a question.

Anecdotal records are brief stories or narratives of seemingly important events. They can deal with feelings as well as facts. When they describe the setting, time of day, students involved, and precipitating circumstances, anecdotal records provide a rich data base for identifying trends. Keeping anecdotal records of both typical and unusual behaviors for a student or group is best. When using open-ended strategies for collecting data such as writing anecdotal records, avoid bias by using only objective language in your reports. For example, it implies a judgment to say in an anecdotal report: "The student was enthusiastic about the lesson." Instead, an observation should use specific, observable facts, such as: "The student waved his hand in response to every question asked." Learning to use this type of descriptive language will enable you to withhold judgment until you have enough data to see true trends and to understand students more completely.

In any type of observation, maintaining a student's right to confidentiality and privacy is important. Avoid inappropriate discussion or identification of students.

Assessing through Processfolios and Learning Journals

Processfolios and learning journals are two techniques enabling learners to focus as much on how they are learning as on what they are learning. They both require deliberate reflections to identify trends and insights about learning.

PROCESSFOLIOS   A processfolio is a collection of all the documents generated from the different stages of a project (Gardner, 1993). It includes notes, ideas, questions, and drafts. A processfolio is best organized longitudinally with the time sequence clearly indicated. The processfolio is valuable because it allows students to reflect on the path their studies have taken. However, unless time and guidance for reflection are given by the teacher, processfolios can become burdensome accumulations of paper. Therefore, processfolios are best used when classes try new methods of investigating or studying and the process itself warrants careful study.

LEARNING JOURNALS   Learning journals are intended to engage students in writing about what they have learned. Students should reflect on and analyze their learning rather than just describe their learning. At their best, learning journals provide a record of student construction of understanding, with fully apparent pathways and processes.

One form of journal, called a "dialogue journal," engages teachers and students in a conversation about learning. Dialogue journals help students feel more personally connected to their teacher. Furthermore, teachers can encourage reflectivity and further investigations by asking probing questions and making suggestions.

In addition, journals are often excellent sources of information on feelings about student activities and abilities. When journal information is treated respectfully and confidentially, learners are usually quite candid. Since dialogue journals can be time consuming for teachers, they might opt to have students periodically maintain learning dialogues with classmates.

Assessing through Portfolios

The portfolio, an organized documentation of student learning, portrays academic development over time. When a teacher uses a variety of methods for gathering evidence of student progress, she obviously needs a system to organize that evidence. Student portfolios can meet this need. Teachers can design portfolios in many forms, depending on their purposes. Some portfolios are comprehensive in nature and thus would be designed to show a student's full range of abilities and accomplishments. Other portfolios might be focused on one particular skill area, such as writing or mathematical applications. Likewise, a portfolio might be designed to show the learning occurring for a student during a particular theme study.

Generally, portfolios contain many different types of information submitted by a number of people who know the learner and his work well. The types of assessment appearing in portfolios can include teacher observations, performance assessment tasks, creative writing, formal content tests, standardized tests, self-assessments, and a variety of work samples. All entries in a portfolio are dated and prefaced with a brief explanation of their significance. Maintaining portfolios should not be seen as the sole responsibility of the teachers. Students themselves should be involved in selecting documents for portfolios, rationalizing the significance of documents, filing documents, and reorganizing their portfolios.

Portfolios are a means of providing compelling evidence that students are progressing toward a destination. In order to have a true portfolio system of assessment, that destination must be defined by setting standards or criteria for excellence. Many professional organizations, such as the National Council of Teachers of Mathematics, are working at setting national standards. Likewise, many state departments of education and local school districts are formulating standards. Clearly, the job of the classroom teacher is to connect portfolio work to any relevant state and national standards. In addition, when developing portfolios based on theme studies, the teacher must also connect the portfolio work to the criteria established for performance assessments and to the attainment of the chosen concepts. Thus, portfolio information directly reflects the goals of the curriculum.

Self-Assessments

Students can participate in all aspects of theme studies, including assessment. Evaluating their own progress helps students become autonomous learners. Self-evaluation can take many forms.

A helpful type of self-assessment is an initial survey or interview assessing a student's current understanding of the concepts as well as her learning disposition. This type of assessment instrument is effective for activating the student's prior knowledge. It also provides data on the uniqueness of a particular group. Sample questions about the theme include:

1. What do you know about (theme focus)?
2. When people talk about (theme focus), what do you think they mean?
3. What puzzles you about (theme focus)?

Sample questions about dispositions might include:

4. What kinds of activities do you like best at school?
5. When do you feel like a good learner?
6. When do you work best with other students?

As the theme study progresses, teachers might interview students about other aspects: for example, the manner in which they work as a group. Sample questions about group work include:

7. What did you do to help your team?
8. What accomplishments of your group give you special pride?
9. What were some things that were difficult for your group?

In addition to interviews, teachers can conduct individual and group conferences to promote self-assessment. Often these conferences center on work samples. Students can discuss their work most effectively when they have been given criteria in advance to guide an assessment of their work. Once students understand the criteria, the only prompts they need for evaluating work are usually open-ended questions such as, What comments would you like to make about your project?

Students keeping portfolios are continually evaluating their work and their progress as they select satisfying pieces to add. Processfolios and learning journals also invite students to assess their own learning. Whenever self-assessment is a strong element of a theme study, students can be responsible for knowing where they are, where they are headed, and how they plan to get there.

HOW CAN THE SCHOOL CURRICULUM BE MADE VISIBLE?

To make the school curriculum visible, all teachers in the school should help document and assess the total school curriculum taught through theme studies. They do this in two ways. First, each teacher implementing a theme provides evaluation feedback to the curriculum team writing the study so that important revisions, additions, and refinements to the curriculum can be made. Additionally, after using a Theme Box prepared by a school-based curriculum team, the implementing teacher might suggest new activity ideas, annotations to book lists, bibliography updates, and refinements of performance assessments. Implementing teachers might add teacher-made materials as well as samples of student work.

A second way teachers assess the school curriculum is by generating school-wide data about all the themes taught in the school. Without this school-wide effort to track the most important aspects of all theme studies, duplications and serious omissions will likely occur. Assessment data also need to be shared and analyzed so that the total curriculum is continually improved. Curriculum mapping is an ideal way to assemble this data.

Curriculum Mapping

Teachers should chart the theme studies used in their school. Creating a school-wide curriculum map indicating which theme studies are presently taught and in which particular grades allows teachers to develop this big picture. Jacobs (1997) offers a process for mapping all subjects in the curriculum. Jacobs defines curriculum mapping as follows:

> Curriculum mapping is a procedure for collecting data about the actual curriculum in a school district using the school calendar as an organizer. Data is gathered in a format allowing each teacher to present an overview of his or her students' actual learning experiences. The fundamental purpose of mapping is communication. The composite of each teacher's map in a building or district provides efficient access to a K–12 curriculum perspective both vertically and horizontally. Mapping is not presented as what "ought" to happen but what "is" happening during the course of a school year. Data offers an overview rather than a daily classroom perspective. Curriculum mapping is an extremely useful tool for creating a "big picture" for curriculum decision making (p. 61).

While Jacobs proposes a model for all curriculum, we are focusing here only on procedures for mapping theme studies. Her model works well for schools using an integrated curriculum. Jacobs recommends that curriculum maps be established by calendar month and indicate content, skills, and important assessments. Using a composite of this data from all implemented theme studies, a school faculty could determine gaps, redundancies, and adjustments needed in theme studies. This form of curriculum mapping also makes it possible to determine whether standards and required skills are being addressed in a balanced way. Furthermore, the data will indicate whether a variety of types of products and performances are used in performance assessments or whether a few types, such as written or oral reports, are overused. Not only will this data assist in revising the array of existing theme studies, it will help in setting the direction for new theme studies. In the process Jacobs suggests, individual teachers would be responsible for submitting data based on what they actually taught in their theme studies by completing a calendar-based map. Figure 7.7 shows a sample of data that a second grade teacher might submit for the theme studies taught during one semester. Action Pack 7-9 is a form to be used by classroom teachers engaged in mapping the curriculum.

Figure 7.7 *Sample Grade 2 Integrated Curriculum Map*

Month	Theme Study Parameters	Skills	Assessments
September	**Nearby Places:** *Our School*		
	Concepts: 1. A school depends on everyone assuming responsibility as a group member. 2. A school depends on mutual respect. 3. A school needs rules.	mapping skills	create a 2-dimensional map of the school
		writing skills: writing informational piece with relevant illustrations	write a student guide for new students to the school
	Guiding Question: How can we share this place for learning?	active listening skills	conduct a classroom meeting for problem solving
October	**Nearby Places:** *Our Community*		
	Concepts: 1. Each community has a unique heritage and customs. 2. Communities grow and change. 3. There are 3 main types of communities: rural, urban, and suburban. 4. Community jobs depend on natural resources. 5. Communities help people meet their basic needs.	mapping skills	design a 2- or 3-dimensional map of the community
		writing skills: writing informational piece showing description	create a brochure on the community to be distributed through the local chamber of commerce
		oral language skills: showing logical progression of ideas	create an informational video on the community
	Guiding questions: What is unique about our community? Who helps our community?		

Figure 7.7 (continued)

Month	Theme Study Parameters	Skills	Assessments
November	**Places Far Away:** *American Desert*		
	Concepts: **1.** The desert is a geographic region with its own climate, land forms, and natural resources. **2.** All living and non-living parts of the desert are linked together in a naturally functioning ecosystem that must be preserved. **3.** A wide variety of plant life is uniquely adapted to the desert. **4.** Animal species that live in the desert are survivors of natural selection and are adapted to life there. **5.** The desert is home to a diversity of people whose cultures have been influenced by the climate, land forms, and natural resources.	mapping skills reading skills: identifying main ideas and supporting details researching skills: finding relevant factual information	map out a trip to the American Desert create a graphic organizer that compares the American Desert and the local community create animal picture/fact cards
	Guiding Question: How is the American desert like my home? How is the American desert different from my home?		

When teachers make available all data about all the themes presently studied in the school, they will be more fully informed about the total experiences of the students. Using this data, which can be easily maintained on computers, all the teachers in the school can participate in evaluating the curricular big picture.

The following story illustrates what can happen when schools implement themes studies without school-wide coordination, such as curriculum mapping.

> DOROTHY: *One of our recent graduates was beginning her first teaching position and decided to implement a theme study on butterflies, a topic of interest to her and her students. Several teachers in the next grade level became quite angry with her because they routinely conducted a theme study on the same topic. The new teacher was distraught both about getting off to a bad start with her colleagues and almost creating a curriculum redundancy. Unfortunately, in this school the system for communicating among teachers about theme studies was extremely informal and allowed this kind of misunderstanding to occur.*

CONCLUSION

Assessing theme studies involves making visible both the learning of students in individual classes and the curriculum decisions within the entire school. What learners know and can do may be demonstrated in a variety of ways other than traditional content tests. These options include performance assessments, teacher observations, processfolios, learning journals, portfolios, and self-assessment. Many assessment decisions are best made early in the planning process of a theme study. Curriculum teams participate in this early planning by developing optional performance assessments that address concepts and guiding questions. Curriculum mapping is an effective, school-wide technique for communicating the thematic curriculum.

Chapter 8 describes additional resources that a curriculum team can develop to supplement the essential parameters of the theme study.

BRAINSTORMING PERFORMANCE ASSESSMENTS

AP7-1

Brainstorming Rules

1. Accept all ideas
No discussion or debate is acceptable.

2. Encourage quantity
Spontaneous and unusual ideas are welcome.

3. Organize at the end
Edit ideas by synthesizing, improving, or eliminating.

Theme Focus:

Concepts

1.

2.

3.

4.

5.

Guiding Questions

1.

2.

3.

Brainstormed Performance Assessments

Promising Options

List the four or five performance assessments that your team judges to be promising.

1.

2.

3.

4.

5.

Evaluate the Options

From the list above, choose two assessment possibilities that best answer each question below. Write the corresponding number on the lines.

Which of these choices:

Best reflect what we want our students to be able to do?   _____   _____

Most directly focus on the guiding questions?   _____   _____

Would be impossible to do unless the concepts were well understood?   _____   _____

Best require application, analysis, and synthesis of the theme content?   _____   _____

Best reflect real-world application of knowledge?   _____   _____

Require skills that are appropriate and valuable for our students?   _____   _____

Are challenging and yet developmentally appropriate?   _____   _____

Are most worth the time and effort required to complete?   _____   _____

Select Your Options

As a team, compare the answers to the questions above and use them to select the two most promising performance assessments.

1.

2.

DRAFTING PERFORMANCE ASSESSMENT DESCRIPTIONS

Write an outline for each of your performance assessment choices. As you work through the remaining steps, your conceptualization may change. You will write a final descriptive paragraph after following the remaining steps.

Assessment One:

Assessment Two:

BRAINSTORMING ENRICHMENT POSSIBILITIES USING GARDNER'S MULTIPLE INTELLIGENCES

 **AP7-4**

Brainstorm activity ideas that show how the performance assessment might allow students to use a number of the multiple intelligences as described by Gardner (1993):

1. Verbal linguistic

2. Logical mathematical

3. Visual spatial

4. Bodily kinesthetic

5. Musical

6. Interpersonal

7. Intrapersonal

8. Naturalistic

Note: Make duplicates of this page for each performance assessment under consideration.

Determine learning outcomes or content goals for the performance assessment. Begin by listing the concepts addressed by the performance assessment and add any additional outcomes or goals. Ask the question: What lasting knowledge and understanding do we want children to demonstrate through this performance assessment?

Examples: Students will compare similarities and differences of two cultures.

Students will understand how geography affects the development of a culture.

List of Content Goals:

Note: Make duplicates of this page for each performance assessment under consideration.

Determine the broad learning outcomes that are process or skill goals for this performance assessment. Remember to consider thinking, creative, social, literacy, and mathematical skills and processes. Ask the question: What skills and processes do we want children to demonstrate through this performance assessment?

Examples: Students will demonstrate persuasive communication skills.

Students will organize work effectively with partners.

Now review state and district standards to determine if there are additional important required skills and processes that should be imbedded into this assessment. If so, add these to your list.

List of Process and Skill Goals:

Note: Make duplicates of this page for each performance assessment under consideration.

Use this format to type a final description of the performance assessment.

Theme Focus:

Guiding Questions:

Performance Assessment Description: (Using Action Packs 7-3 and 7-4, write a descriptive paragraph of the performance assessment.)

Content Goals: (Using Action Pack 7-5, write final content goals.)

Process and Skill Goals: (Using Action Pack 7-6, write final process and skill goals.)

Note: Make duplicates of this page for each performance assessment under consideration.

Activity No. _____

Activity Name: _____

Materials Needed:

Activity Description:

Possible Adaptations (if appropriate):

Citation (if appropriate):

Contributed by: _____

Use this format to document activities to support your content, skill, and process goals and to engage children in using their multiple intelligences. The number of activity ideas will vary depending on the performance assessment selected.

Grade: _____

Month	Theme Study Parameters	Skills	Assessments

Directions: Submit data on theme studies actually taught by completing this calendar-based map.

CHAPTER 8

Developing Supplemental Resources

GUIDING QUESTIONS

How Do Curriculum Teams Develop Supplemental Resources?
How Can Curriculum Teams Be Productive and Efficient?

A curriculum writing team spends the majority of its time creating a resource book or curriculum guide for teachers. Since a theme resource guide defines the essential parameters of the theme study, a curriculum writing team gives priority to establishing the theme focus, concept statements, guiding questions, content summary, and performance assessments. However, many teams opt to go beyond these minimum requirements by collaboratively developing additional resources for implementing teachers.

HOW DO CURRICULUM TEAMS DEVELOP SUPPLEMENTAL RESOURCES?

Resources that curriculum teams may choose to develop for their Theme Box include graphic organizers, activity ideas, glossaries, teacher-made materials, bibliographies, web site resources, and artifact collections. Figure 8.1 gives many suggestions for your Theme Box resources.

Graphic Organizers

By now your team knows what it deems to be the most important content for the theme study. The team has summarized this content for classroom teachers in reports, webs, and lists of content questions. However,

Figure 8.1 *Theme Box Content Suggestions*

Basic:

Theme Resource Book
Theme-Related Literature

Supplemental Options (Purchased and/or Teacher-Made)

Purchased Theme Units

Literature-Related Resources: kits or individual pieces including activity books, teacher guides, manipulatives, pictures

Music: CDs, cassettes, videos, songbooks, instruments

Computer Software: programs, games, PowerPoint presentations, clip art collections, related web site lists, directed Internet searches

Presentation Aids: transparencies, graphic organizers, charts, posters, maps, models

Bulletin Board Materials: plans, bulletin board pieces, borders

Theme-Related Collections: poetry, riddles, jokes, story starters, pictures, recipes, postcards, stamps, bookmarks

Manipulatives: puppets, flannel graph pieces, paper dolls, cutouts

Models: dolls, cars, animals, planets

Games: card, board, file folder, matching, twister, memory

Puzzles: picture, crossword, word searches, scavenger hunts

Cards: biography, flash, fact, culture, picture

Costumes and Dress Up: clothes, hats, shoes, masks, props

Arts and Crafts: rubber stamps, lacing cards, painting sponges

Room Decorations: pictures, mobiles, signs, art reproductions, dioramas, posters

Artifacts: nests, seeds, thermometers, insect collections, stuffed birds, tools, instruments, barometers, magnets, chop sticks, sea shells

Kits: discovery, pretend, craft, dress up, chemistry

Background Information Materials: sample lesson plans, magazine articles, bibliographies

Sample Student Work: journals, stories, pictures, videos, projects

---

students are helped by having the theme content graphically represented for them. A graphic organizer is a visual representation of the connections between interrelated ideas. Graphic organizers depict the structure among important ideas and make their relative importance clear. They also highlight and therefore focus attention on the most important ideas while subsuming related supporting aspects.

Graphic organizers serve a variety of purposes when used with learners. When graphic organizers present ideas that are already known to students in relationship to new ideas, they provide a framework for assimilating new knowledge. When graphic organizers focus on important terminology, they clarify defining characteristics or attributes of the concept. When used in an initiating activity, they provide an advance organizer for students and thus facilitate remembering as well as understanding. During closure activities, they return students to the big picture. Graphic organizers promote higher level thinking because they focus on the interrelationships among ideas. Graphic organizers can also assess learning by requiring students to supply missing information. The ultimate goal is to equip students to design their own organizers that map their understandings. In summary, graphic organizers are tools that enable learners to (1) discover patterns and connections between ideas; (2) distinguish between major ideas and supporting ideas; and (3) communicate the structure among concepts.

TYPES OF GRAPHIC ORGANIZERS   Five main types of organizers are especially helpful to students: classification, hierarchical, conceptual, sequential, and cyclical.

Classification organizers put information into categories to facilitate comparisons. Figure 8.2 is an example of an interactive organizer

Figure 8.2   *Sample Interactive Classification Organizer*

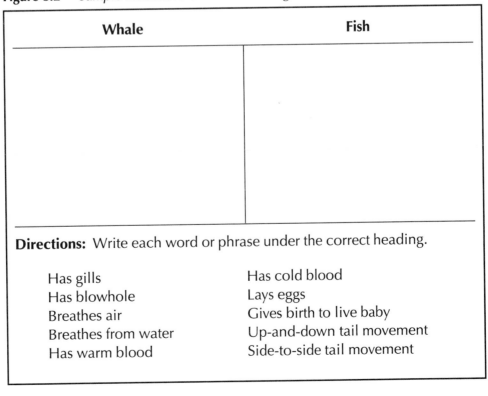

Whale	**Fish**

Directions: Write each word or phrase under the correct heading.

Has gills	Has cold blood
Has blowhole	Lays eggs
Breathes air	Gives birth to live baby
Breathes from water	Up-and-down tail movement
Has warm blood	Side-to-side tail movement

comparing whales and fish. Figure 8.3 makes a time comparison to enable students to better understand a theme on the *Titanic.* Another example of classification organizers is a Venn diagram comparing two phenomena having overlapping attributes. Figure 8.4 is a sample comparing farm and wild animals. A matrix is also a type of classification organizer showing a number of categories that are compared by looking at important variables. Figure 8.5 compares variables for a theme on American heroines.

Hierarchical organizers present a main concept with ranks or levels of subconcepts. The phylum of the animal kingdom or a family tree would be presented this way. Another example of a hierarchical orga-

Figure 8.3   *Sample Classification Organizer for* Titanic *Theme*

1912	Present
The tragic event was believed avoidable.	The tragic event was proved avoidable.
Proper crew training was not provided.	Law requires proper training of crew.
The *Titanic's* crew did not have the technology that exists today.	Up-to-date technology and equipment are used.
The *Titanic* did not carry a sufficient number of lifeboats.	A sufficient number of lifeboats is required.
Priority was given to first- and second-class passengers during emergency.	All passengers are given equal attention during an emergency.
The crew disregarded communications.	Stable communications are maintained.
No boat safety drill was conducted and guns were used for crowd control.	A safety drill is required and emergency procedures are followed.
The first and second class enjoyed all the luxuries of the ship while third class had few.	All passengers are welcome to use all the luxuries that a ship offers.
The *Titanic* settled two miles below the Atlantic's surface, and wasn't found for decades.	The *Titanic* is explored underwater, where it lies two miles below the Atlantic's surface.

Figure 8.4   *Sample Venn Diagram for a Farm Theme*

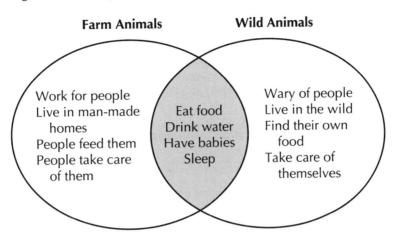

nizer is an outline. Figure 8.6 is an example of a hierarchy depicting part of the animal kingdom phylum.

Conceptual organizers are appropriate for conveying information where a central idea is supported with facts, characteristics, or examples that cannot be ranked in levels. An example of a conceptual organizer would be a web such as the one in Figure 8.7 on camping safety.

Figure 8.5   *Sample Matrix for Theme on American Heroines*

Characteristics of American Heroines			
Summary Matrix			
Characteristics	**Name**		
	Science **Elizabeth Blackwell**	*Social Science* **Rosa Parks**	*Sports* **Babe Didrickson**	*Fine Arts* **Dat-so-la-lee**
Dedication	X	X	X	X
Perseverance	X	X	X	X
Physical courage			X	
Moral courage	X	X		X
Goal-oriented	X	X	X	X
Service-oriented	X			X
Strong work ethic	X	X	X	X

Figure 8.6 *Sample Hierarchical Graphic Organizer*

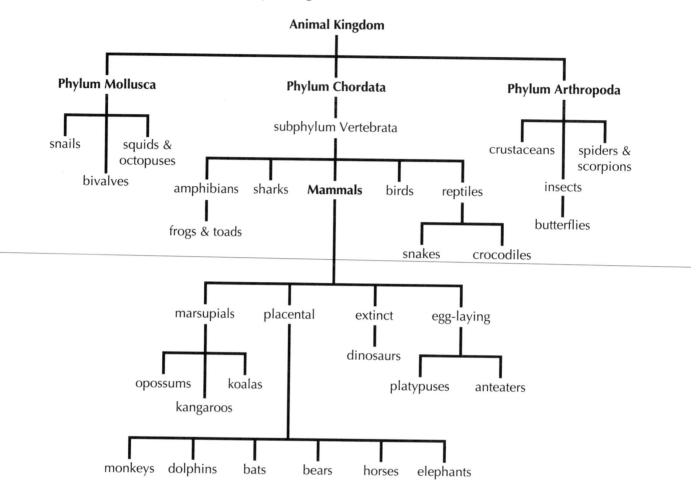

Sequential organizers arrange events in a logical order. Examples include time lines, cause and effect diagrams, numbered steps or ladders, and mazes with definite beginning and end points. A timeline for the sinking of the *Titanic* provides an example in Figure 8.8. A hurricane sequence for a theme study on natural disasters provides another example in Figure 8.9.

Cyclical organizers are appropriate for a continuous sequence of events with no discernible beginning and end. Figure 8.10 is an example of the weather cycle in the African grasslands that causes animals to migrate.

PROCESS FOR DESIGNING GRAPHIC ORGANIZERS   Teams we have worked with recommend two alternative approaches to creating graphic organizers. The first approach involves studying the important information you wish to illustrate and searching for the most appropriate type of graphic organizer. Action Pack 8-1 will assist you when

Figure 8.7 *Sample Conceptual Organizer about Camping Safety*

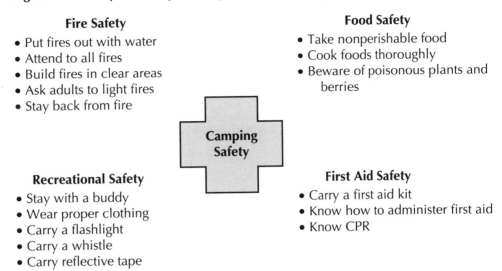

Fire Safety
- Put fires out with water
- Attend to all fires
- Build fires in clear areas
- Ask adults to light fires
- Stay back from fire

Food Safety
- Take nonperishable food
- Cook foods thoroughly
- Beware of poisonous plants and berries

Camping Safety

Recreational Safety
- Stay with a buddy
- Wear proper clothing
- Carry a flashlight
- Carry a whistle
- Carry reflective tape

First Aid Safety
- Carry a first aid kit
- Know how to administer first aid
- Know CPR

using this approach. An alternative strategy is to review each graphic organizer type and determine whether you have significant material that could be presented in this format. Use Action Pack 8-2 to assist you with this approach.

Once you know what kind of information you want to present graphically, you can choose an appropriate type of organizer for highlighting the existing connections. After you design the basic structure of the organizer, consider ways to make it more appealing and developmentally appropriate for your students. For example: Can it be designed

Figure 8.8 *Sample Time Line for the* Titanic *Theme*

Time Line for 1912 Sinking of the *Titanic*

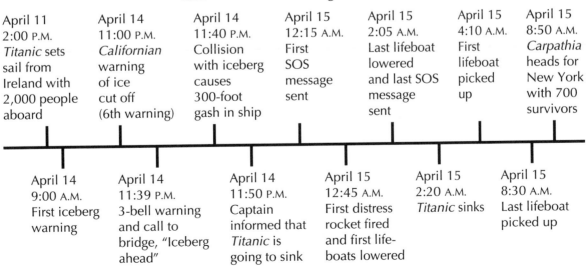

April 11
2:00 P.M.
Titanic sets sail from Ireland with 2,000 people aboard

April 14
11:00 P.M.
Californian warning of ice cut off (6th warning)

April 14
11:40 P.M.
Collision with iceberg causes 300-foot gash in ship

April 15
12:15 A.M.
First SOS message sent

April 15
2:05 A.M.
Last lifeboat lowered and last SOS message sent

April 15
4:10 A.M.
First lifeboat picked up

April 15
8:50 A.M.
Carpathia heads for New York with 700 survivors

April 14
9:00 A.M.
First iceberg warning

April 14
11:39 P.M.
3-bell warning and call to bridge, "Iceberg ahead"

April 14
11:50 P.M.
Captain informed that *Titanic* is going to sink

April 15
12:45 A.M.
First distress rocket fired and first lifeboats lowered

April 15
2:20 A.M.
Titanic sinks

April 15
8:30 A.M.
Last lifeboat picked up

Figure 8.9   *Sample Sequential Organizer for Hurricanes from Start to Finish*

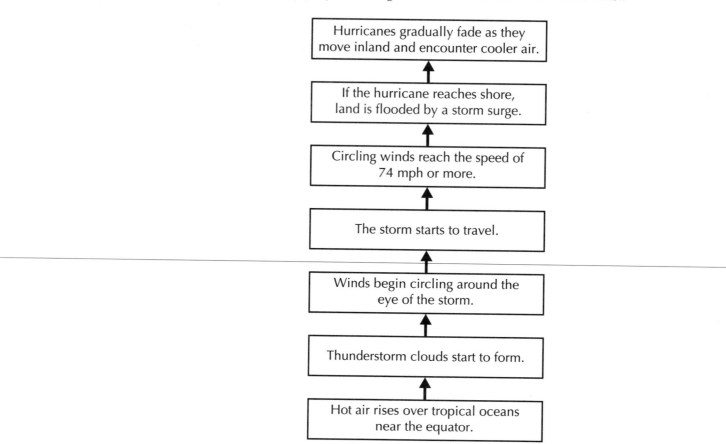

to be interactive? Can pictures or three-dimensional objects be used to represent the main ideas? What would be the most appealing media for the graphic organizer: a picture chart, flannel set, magnetic board, or overhead transparency?

Graphic organizers are only one type of valuable supplemental resource. Many teams choose to devote entire sections of the resource book to alternative activity ideas.

Activity Sections

Teams choosing to accept the challenge of generating a wide variety of optional activity ideas to include in their resource guides often find this to be one of the most enjoyable theme building aspects. Teams can generate their own activities and collect published activities ideas as soon as a focus is identified. However, it is advisable to postpone selection of the activities to be included in the Theme Box. At first, you might be tempted to include all interesting activity ideas in your resource book. However, with many theme hubs, the number of poten-

Figure 8.10   *A Cyclical Organizer for an African Grasslands Theme*

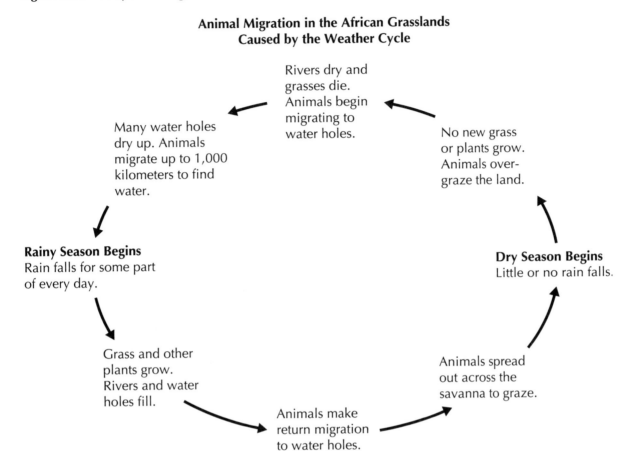

**Animal Migration in the African Grasslands
Caused by the Weather Cycle**

Rivers dry and grasses die. Animals begin migrating to water holes.

Many water holes dry up. Animals migrate up to 1,000 kilometers to find water.

No new grass or plants grow. Animals overgraze the land.

Rainy Season Begins
Rain falls for some part of every day.

Dry Season Begins
Little or no rain falls.

Grass and other plants grow. Rivers and water holes fill.

Animals spread out across the savanna to graze.

Animals make return migration to water holes.

tial activity ideas can be overwhelming. In addition, the team cannot discern the best activities to include until concepts and guiding questions are developed to give cohesiveness and substance to the theme study. The team also needs to agree on quality standards for activity ideas.

OPTIONS FOR ACTIVITY SECTIONS   Many teams find that having an activity section for each concept statement makes the most sense. Other groups may develop activity sections along different content lines. For example, one team writing a resource unit on transportation created activity sections related to land transportation, air transportation, and water transportation. Other teams may use activity sections following discipline lines, including a creative arts section, a language arts section, and a math/science section. Teams choosing discipline-based sections are reminded that many activities address overlapping disciplines and may not fit neatly under a specific discipline area. The team must find ways to include these integrated activities. In schools embracing Gardner's multiple intelligences theory, curriculum teams might want to organize sections of activity ideas around the intelligences. In addition to these major activity sections, some teams include collections of poetry, jokes, fingerplays, songs, or recipes. When choosing activities, remember that they should support your concepts, guiding questions, and performance assessments. Our teams have found some sections to be especially valuable to implementing teachers: concept-based activities, read and respond activities, sponge activities, and long-term project activities.

Concept-Based Activity Sections. A common and effective way to organize activity ideas is around the chosen concept statements. Organizing activity ideas in this way helps guarantee that instruction time is focused on the important parameters of a theme study: concepts, guiding questions, and performance assessments. Figure 8.11 shows one way to organize activity ideas around a chosen concept statement for a theme study on African grasslands. Please be sure to notice that activity ideas addressing more than one concept require a special notation.

Read and Respond Activity Sections. A review of theme-related literature will suggest many creative activity ideas. For most themes, the team should purchase several pieces of literature for the Theme Box. Chosen literature should meet standards of quality, provide enjoyment for learners, and help students understand the concepts. Designing activities around your team's literature choices is a profitable way to generate purposeful learning experiences. Read and respond activities should engage students in meaningful learning that maximizes the connections between the piece of literature and the theme. Every effort should be made to design activities that learners find enjoyable and relevant. Read and respond activities often provide opportunities for self-expression and give choices to learners. Figure 8.12 provides several read and respond activities based on *The Cloud Book* by Tomie dePaola (1975).

Teams relying entirely on the selected literature for activity ideas and for ways of teaching concepts are using what is called by Allen and Piersma (1995) the "literature infused model." Although he doesn't use this term, Thompson (1991) explains this model in depth and provides examples.

Sponge Activity Sections. Teams may also choose to develop a collection of "sponge" activities (Hunter, 1994) for mopping up spare moments in the day. We define sponge activities as individual, goal-oriented work focusing spare transition minutes on productive learning. Effective sponge activities should be educationally worthwhile,

Figure 8.11 *Sample Activity Plan Organized around a Concept*

Concept Activity Section

Guiding Questions:

How is a child's life in the African grasslands different from a child's life in Pennsylvania?
How is a child's life in the African grasslands similar to a child's life in Pennsylvania?

Concept Statement:

A wide variety of animals, many unique to the African grasslands, roam freely on the savanna. A great number of these are endangered.

Activities	Materials	Assessment
1. Research an African animal. Make a collector plate of that animal with a picture on the front and four animal facts on the back.	Paper plates, markers, construction paper, variety of books on African animals	Accuracy of students' four written facts about the chosen animal; a complete picture of an animal for each plate.
Discuss how these animals are similar to and different from local animals.	Comparison chart on similarities and differences between lives in two environments	Observation of students' responses.
2. Discuss the problem of poachers. Have children identify what endangered animals are and what we can do to save them.	Dictionary, pictures of endangered African animals, poacher and animal puppets	Children's oral responses to questions about endangered animals; oral and written identifications of African animals; Teacher observation as pairs of children use their poacher and animal puppets to talk to each other.
3. Read African folktale, create a short play; make animal masks and perform play. Compare African folktale to American tall tale. (Relates to concept 4)	The book, *Who's in Rabbit's House*, paper bags, markers, scissors, variety of materials for props Companion chart	Optional Performance Assessments: Written dialogue drawn from story; oral responses to questions about order and identification of animals in story; masks that resemble animals; ability to perform play.
4. Invent an African folktale using researched facts about African animals; devise plot for folktale focusing on endangerment.	Research materials, writing materials	Optional performance assessment: Authenticity of writing in folktale genre, integration of factual content about animals and endangerment.

195

Figure 8.12   *Sample of a Read and Respond Activity*

Title: *The Cloud Book*   **Author:** Tomie dePaola

Illustrator: Tomie dePaola   **Publisher & Date:** Holiday House, 1975

Type of Book: Informational Fiction   **Grade/Age Level:** Primary

Summary: This is a book of myths and facts about clouds. Interspersed throughout the book are many basic facts about clouds including types of clouds, indications about the weather, and ways that they are formed. In addition, the book includes different cultural views of clouds.

Illustrations: The illustrations are a mixture of fantasy cloud pictures with factual drawings to help children identify the different types of clouds they see.

Theme Connection: The weather in the African grasslands consists of a wet and dry season. Rain is critically important and controls the lives of both animals and humans. Learning to understand clouds and what they tell us about the weather is an important skill for many people living in the grasslands.

Possible Response Activities:

1. Cloud Sightings

Materials: *The Cloud Book* and Journals

Procedures: Share *The Cloud Book* with your class. On a cloudy day, go outside to observe the sky. Have learners record what they see in their journals. They may want to sketch the cloud shapes and describe them.

2. Cloud Stories

Materials: Journal observations (from no.1) and chart paper or writing material

Procedures: Using journal observations from the cloud-sighting activity, students will create stories about: (1) shapes they saw in the clouds, (2) ways they would feel if they were a cloud, or (3) things clouds would see from the sky if clouds could see.

3. Cloud Dances

Materials: Journal observations (from no.1) and white sheets or scarves

Procedures: Using observations from journals, children choreograph a creative movement or dance routine to reflect the movement of clouds through the sky.

4. Cloud Pictures

Materials: Journal observations (from no.1), blue construction paper, cotton balls, glue, black water paint or snow paint, and blue or black food coloring

Procedures: Using the descriptions from their journals, students will create pictures of clouds using either cotton balls or snow paint. Use the black or blue paint or food coloring to darken some clouds.

interesting to students, and of short duration. Also, students should be able to do them quietly, independently, and easily. Sponge activities often fall into one of four categories: interactive activities such as bulletin boards, listening centers, or computer work; moments for writing including creative writing, e-mail or letter writing, journal writing, and answering questions of the day; art projects such as drawing pictures or decorating bulletin boards; and games such as matching games, file folder games, board games, puzzles, anagrams, and mazes. Figure 8.13 provides an example of an appropriate sponge activity.

Long-Term Project Activity Sections. Long-term projects take place over several days or even weeks and may have identifiable stages. Many long-term projects are used as performance assessments. However, this is not always the case, as in an extended art project or the production of a play. Long-term projects help teachers move away from lessons that are always geared to a fixed number of minutes. Also, their complexity inevitably requires an integration of the disciplines. Moreover, engaging projects give students a sense of accomplishment and satisfaction. Figure 8.14 provides a sample long-term project for an African grasslands theme.

PROCESS FOR DESIGNING ACTIVITY SECTIONS   Where do activity ideas come from? Often the best ideas come from the creativity of your team. Teams generate unique ideas primarily through brainstorming. However, curriculum teams should also use a full range of resources

Figure 8.13   *Sample Sponge Activity*

Sponge Activity: Weather vs. Climate

Materials: 3 × 5 cards & markers

Procedures: On two 3 × 5 cards, make category cards by writing the words "weather" and "climate." On additional 3 × 5 cards (possibly of a different color), write words or phrases that describe weather and climate. Students will match these description cards with the correct category card and make a classification board. This could also be made into an interactive bulletin board. Emphasis should be placed on weather as something happening today and climate as a weather pattern that prevails over an extended time period.

Some examples for description cards include:

weather—72 degrees today, sunny, rainy, hot, cold

climate—average temperature ranges between 72 and 84 degrees, dry season, rainy season, average rainfall of 60 inches annually

---

when assembling ideas, including published resource books, professional journals, Internet web sites, and other teachers.

Brainstorming Activities Using Planning Organizers. You can facilitate a productive flow of creative ideas for activities and experiences by using the planning webs provided in Action Packs 8-3 to 8-9. Each planning web invites you to look at your focus in a fresh way by presenting different possibilities. Using a planning web with organizing categories is a simple procedure. For example, if you are working with the theme focus "Our National Parks: A Camping Trip" you might choose to work with a planning web on the five senses. You would put the theme focus in the hub and ask yourself the question: If the students were actually to visit the national parks, what might they smell, taste, see, touch, and hear? Follow the rules for brainstorming and list all ideas without prejudging them. Achieving an equal number of ideas in each category is not important, while giving conscious attention to each possible category is critical. Figure 8.15 provides an example of a planning organizer

Figure 8.14 *Sample Long-Term Project*

Long Term Project: Shadow Play of *Who's in Rabbit's House,* by Verna Aardema (Dial Press, 1977)

Materials: *Who's in Rabbit's House* (if possible, supply multiple copies) brown grocery bags and markers for masks
large cardboard box to make hut

Procedures: Read *Who's in Rabbit's House* together as a class. Discuss the illustrations, Masaii actors wearing animal masks, by Leo and Diane Dillon. Group students as actors, readers, and production team members.

The actors will each be assigned a character from the book. Using the grocery bags and markers, they will each make a mask to wear in the shadow play. Each actor will study the actions of his animal and practice the interactions with other characters. The readers will use the book as a basis to write a short play. The readers will practice their lines, using their voices to sound like the animal characters. After practicing independently, readers will practice together until each is sure when to read his or her part. The production team will make a hut using the large cardboard box and any other desired scenery or props.

The three groups will come together for two or three rehearsals until the play runs smoothly. Videotape the play. Students can take turns taking the videotape home to share with their families. If time permits, the students will also enjoy putting on a public performance of their play for family, other classes, and school administration.

Figure 8.15   *Sample of a Brainstorming Web Based on the Five Senses*

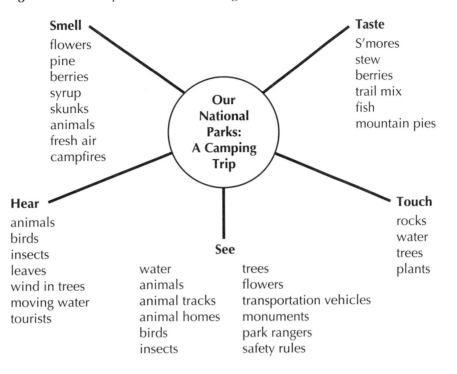

for brainstorming around the five senses. In classes where students could actually visit a national park, teachers would be sure to capitalize on these sensory experiences. Where visits are not possible, teachers could bring many of these sensory experiences into the classroom through audio and video tapes, pictures, interactive programs, simulated experiences, food activities, and artifacts from nature.

Your team may also want to brainstorm activity ideas using literature you have chosen for your Theme Box. Action Pack 8-10 offers ways to brainstorm ideas for pieces of theme-related literature. Action Pack 8-11 provides a sample format to document read and respond activity ideas.

Gathering your own ideas first through brainstorming before delving into resource materials will increase your sense of ownership in the resource unit. Your ideas are valuable because you know best your students, their prior knowledge, and your community. You also know the scope of your particular theme study as defined by the concepts, guiding questions, and chosen performance assessments. Therefore, your ideas generally will be better than those already available in publications. Some teams choose to publish their brainstormed activity webs in the theme resource guide in lieu of preparing paragraph descriptions of selected activity ideas.

Researching Published Resource Materials. After generating their own activities ideas, curriculum writing teams will often search published resources for activity ideas. Published thematic resources vary tremendously in quality. Some will present a shallow focus conceptualization but provide some worthy ideas for effective activities. When your team finds a high quality theme resource on its particular focus, you may want to purchase this guide for the Theme Box. Curriculum team members often adapt specific ideas by combining or using them in fresh ways. The team may also want to include some activity ideas from published sources by quoting or paraphrasing them in its resource unit. When adopting or adapting ideas from another source, you should include a complete citation in your team's resource unit.

Establishing Criteria for Activity Ideas. Before individual team members begin writing activity descriptions, the team as a whole should agree on its definition of a quality activity idea and a quality activity section. Rubrics or lists of criteria should be developed. Several teams developed the sample rubric in Figure 8.16 to define excellent activity sections. With agreed-upon criteria in mind, individual team members can make better choices for each activity section.

You can generate excellent criteria lists or rubrics by working with multiple samples of activity descriptions. The following technique offers simple procedures for developing criteria. As a team, sort activity ideas from several sources into three piles representing poor, average, and excellent activities. Then ignore the average pile. Study the pile of excellent activity ideas and ask what characteristics make these activities exceptional. Then study the pile of poor activities and ask what qualities these activity ideas lack. The answers to these two questions will lead the team in developing a criteria list for excellent theme activities. Action Pack 8-12 will guide you in this process.

Organizing Ideas into Activity Sections. Your time is used most efficiently if everyone on the team explores published learning activity possibilities and writes brief descriptions for team generated activity options. Most teams we worked with found it efficient to collectively agree on the sections to be created and then divide the work by assigning each member one or two activity sections to complete. However, some groups opt to have every team member contribute to every section. This second approach requires much closer ongoing coordination to avoid overlapping or duplicating ideas. As teachers divide the work, they are encouraged to use the full range of sources for activity ideas: brainstormed lists, theme-related literature, Internet web sites, published teacher resources, and professional journals. If possible, team

Figure 8.16 *Sample of a Rubric for an Activity Section*

Exceptional Section

a. More than 24 activities presented
b. 70% or more active-learning, performance-oriented activities
c. 100% developmentally appropriate activities
d. 25% or more of activities adapted for exceptional learners
e. 5 or more original activity ideas
f. 5 or more activities connected to theme-related literature
g. 2 or more long-term projects
h. 4 or more disciplines represented by activities
i. 3 or more resources used
j. 3 or more pictures/clip art
k. 99% perfectly edited
l. 100% of text and graphics computer generated and saved
m. Organization easy to follow with section name on every page

Acceptable

a. 24 activities
b. 60-70% active-learning, performance-oriented activities
c. 100% developmentally appropriate activities
d. 10-25% of activities with adaptations for exceptional learners
e. 3 or 4 original activity ideas
f. 3 or 4 activities connected to theme-related literature
g. 1 or more long-term projects
h. 3 disciplines represented by activities
i. 2 resources used
j. 1 or 2 pictures/clip art
k. 95% or more edited (revisions required)
l. 100% of text computer generated; graphics hand drawn
m. Organization is easy to follow with clearly labeled sections

Revision Needed

a. Fewer than 24 activities
b. Fewer than 60% active-learning, performance-oriented activities
c. Nondevelopmentally appropriate material included
d. 0-10% of activities with adaptations for exceptional learners
e. Fewer than 3 original activity ideas
f. Fewer than 3 activity ideas connected to theme-related literature
g. 0 long-term projects
h. Fewer than 3 major disciplines represented by activities
i. Fewer than 2 resources used
j. 0 pictures/clip art
k. Less than 95% edited
l. Text typed but not saved on computer
m. Organization is difficult to follow or lacking

members should use different libraries for research, so that a wider variety of resources is identified.

Once a teacher has written an activity section, he evaluates his own work against the team-defined standards and then submits it to the team for feedback. Action Pack 8-13 provides a form for authors to use to complete an evaluation of three activity ideas. A peer can evaluate another set of three activities using Action Pack 8-14. Once peer editing is complete, the author or editor then completes the revising and editing of activity descriptions.

Additional Resources

In addition to graphic organizers and activity ideas, curriculum teams can provide a valuable service to implementing teachers by preparing glossaries, bibliographies, and teacher-made materials. The Theme Box can be stocked with carefully selected purchased material, even with a limited budget.

GLOSSARIES   Glossaries can be targeted for learners and/or teachers. Include new, unfamiliar, and important words about your theme. Also, define any words that have a specific meaning in your theme study. For example, the word "star" would mean something quite different in a Solar System Theme Box than in a Theater Theme Box. Include definitions and pronunciation guides when necessary, especially if you are including words from foreign languages. You may also want to include activity ideas for introducing and learning vocabulary words.

BIBLIOGRAPHIES   Bibliographies should include a variety of resources beginning with theme-related literature. To be most helpful, bibliographic entries for this literature should be annotated with a short description of the book, the connection to the theme, special features, age appropriateness, and any awards received. Figure 8.17 provides a sample of some annotated entries.

You might include the listings of current titles that you were unable to review, either by indicating they were not reviewed in the annotation or by reprinting an annotation from another source. Annotations of theme-related literature can be found in *Book Review Digest*, the Library of Congress's *Cataloging in Publications Data*, and various Internet web sites.

Your annotated bibliography should also include resource books, films, videos, music, magazines, teaching kits, computer software, web site addresses, and other on-line computer sources. Include community resources whenever possible. Your team should agree on a common style for organizing bibliographical information. Many teams divide the

Figure 8.17 *Sample Annotated Bibliography Entries*

Folklore:

Aardema, Verna. (1971). *Why Mosquitoes Buzz in People's Ears*. New York: Dial. An African folktale introducing many grassland animals and illustrated using African masks. 1976 Caldecott Winner

Aardema, Verna. (1981). *Bringing the Rain to Kapiti Plain: A Nandi Tale*. New York: Dial. An African folktale about what one little cattle-herder did to end drought and bring rain. The entire book is in rhyme.

Greaves, Nick. (1993). *When Lion Could Fly & Other Tales from Africa*. New York: Barrons. Folklore centered around African animals and science facts. A good book to integrate language arts and science.

Nonfiction:

Feelings, Murial. (1972). *jambo means hello: Swahili Alphabet Book*. New York: Dial. An alphabet introducing Swahili words and scenes. The illustrations by Tom Feelings are unique and students may want to try the technique. 1973 Caldecott Winner

Musgrove, Margaret. (1976). *Ashanti to Zulu: African Traditions*. New York: Dial. A beautifully illustrated alphabet book introducing twenty-six different African tribes with short paragraphs on their cultures. 1977 Caldecott Winner

Resource Books:

Jinkins, Barbara. (1993). *Pineapples, Penguins, and Pagodas*. Nashville, TN: Incentive Publications. A resource book including ideas for a year-long educational tour around the world with several learning activities centered around Africa.

---

work of preparing bibliographies by assigning each member a different local library.

PURCHASED MATERIALS Many Theme Box materials are purchased, such as theme-related books, puppets, charts, maps, videos, computer programs, compact disks, games, and tools for learning, such as scientific apparatus. In addition, teams should store collections of artifacts and pictures in the Theme Box. Furthermore, teams might purchase some of the teacher resource books that have been published for many of the common themes studied in both elementary and middle schools.

Some theme-related guides are specifically directed to the use of computers and the Internet in the classroom. Included in these computer resource guides are theme-related, teacher-approved web sites, directed web searches, scavenger hunts, and computer projects.

TEACHER-MADE MATERIALS   As team members reflect on possible theme activities, assessments, and graphic organizers, they will have many ideas for valuable teacher-made materials. Handmade creative teaching materials include games, puzzles, puppets, bulletin board pieces, charts, and flannelgraph sets. Many teams enjoy making teaching materials. We recommend that teachers who opt to create something for the Theme Box also supply a description, directions for making the material, and possible ways to use it. As always, team members should self-evaluate and then peer edit their creations. Figure 8.18 provides a sample format for a creative teaching material description.

Figure 8.18   *Sample Format for Teacher-Made Materials Directions*

Theme: **Name of Creator:**

_____   _____

Name of Creation: **Recommended Ages:**

_____   _____

Materials Needed:
Include a complete list of supplies needed to make the teaching material. Where appropriate, specify quantities and sizes.

Directions:
Include step-by-step directions for making the creative teaching material. Strive for clarity, using illustrations if they would help. Offer any hints you discovered that would make the tasks simpler.

Purposes:
Describe as many ways as possible to use these materials in the course of the theme study.

Possible Adaptations:
Indicate possible adaptations for other age groups and for exceptional learners. You might also include suggestions for relating this material to other concepts or themes.

Note: Where appropriate, attach patterns to this page.

Figure 8.19 provides criteria for excellent teacher-made materials to help with self and peer evaluations. Use Action Pack 8-15 when designing creative teaching materials and Action Pack 8-16 when evaluating them.

HOW CAN CURRICULUM WRITING TEAMS BE PRODUCTIVE AND EFFICIENT?

As teams that we worked with compared notes about the process of developing supplemental resources, they found that they had made many similar errors and explored some of the same dead ends. Their experiences can help other teams to save steps. Experienced curriculum writing teams offer several pieces of advice to others engaged in the process of developing thematic resource materials.

Use Computer Assistance

Because revisions are inevitable, a curriculum writing team is advised to keep its resource guide book on a computer disk. Investigate the capabilities of computer programs available at your school, as well as at local and university libraries. The time spent in becoming acquainted with these options will be well spent. You will be able to make additions and revisions more conveniently if a common school computer is used. When team members use home computers, they should try to use compatible word processing programs.

> LINDA: *While working on this book, Dorothy and I learned the hard way that using compatible word processing programs can eliminate unnecessary work. First drafts of some chapters had to be retyped. We*

Figure 8.19 *Sample Criteria List for Teacher-Made Materials*

1. Attractive with visual impact
2. Versatile, allowing for adaptations
3. Related to theme concepts
4. Developmentally appropriate
5. Durable and safe
6. Simple in design
7. Works as intended
8. Interactive and engaging for students
9. Precise, clear, complete directions

had to do some revisions by hand and we printed a lot of excess paper because we started with different word-processing packages. When we both finally had the same package on our home computers, we were able to trade information on disk and revisions became easier and less time costly.

Using computer assistance and the Internet to research both background reports and activity ideas opens a world of information. If one of your team members is an expert in this area, plan team time for a tutoring session on the use of the Internet. Many libraries and community colleges today will assist you in using this tool efficiently. As you are researching, remember to check web sites for content and age appropriateness for students. This information is valuable later when directing students to age appropriate and exciting links. As students browse through these links, they can access animation, photos, videos, maps, simulations, and valuable texts. Teachers can create directed web searches to be conducted on students' home computers as well as on school computers.

Avoid Retracing Steps

Recording information, activity ideas, or notes on theme-related literature without also recording complete bibliographical citations is an easy mistake to make. Although you can return to a source later for those tasks, retracing is time consuming. A much better approach is to handle a source once, while making complete notes, and printing out source information or downloading the necessary citation. In the end, this attention to detail will save time.

Move Beyond the Obvious

Many researchers hit dry spells when information seems to have evaporated. At times like these, think beyond the obvious. Have you considered magazines, community agencies, museums, zoos, science centers, history centers, videos, films, kits, CD-ROMs, travel agencies, and music and book stores? Another recommendation is to look for tangential materials. Librarians are excellent sources for help in identifying related sources. Additionally, use the bibliographies provided in theme-related teacher resource publications to take advantage of the research of others.

LINDA: *When researching the African grasslands, I found only a few resources when I searched under that specific topic. However, when I expanded my search to include African folktales, weather and rain, and specific animals such as elephants and zebras, I found a large variety of wonderful children's books, poetry, and teacher resources.*

Keep Your Work Organized

Until your theme building project is complete, there will be many pieces of paper to track including rough drafts, ideas, planning forms, and bibliographical information. File papers in an accordion file or a box of labeled hanging files. These can easily be transported to team meetings. You will want to have folders for: (1) each section of the resource book, (2) "ready to publish" versions of your work, (3) each team member, (4) orders placed, and (5) team minutes.

In addition to file folders, stock up on note pads, "post it" notes, and note cards. Information on cards or notes can easily be organized, revised, and shared. Keeping bibliographical information on note cards allows cards to be placed in alphabetical order for easy typing. Some teachers' favorite strategy is strategically placed "post it" notes. Another suggestion for tracking bibliographical information is to start a file on disk, entering each source immediately upon use. If you make annotations as each source is entered, your final bibliography will take little time to complete.

We have worked with curriculum writers who strongly recommended typing in free moments and not postponing this task. Some recommend typing each activity idea as you complete it. Others suggest waiting to type the activity sections until you have gathered and organized all the ideas for a section. All agree that as you complete each section of the resource book, you should create a final publishable product including cover pages and citations. Teams that leave source verifications and citations for the end of the project have trouble finding quickly the information they need. Creating cover pages or section dividers for the resource book can also became a major chore if left till the end. You will find that another benefit in refining and completing each section as you go along is the sense of accomplishment your team feels in seeing completed sections.

CONCLUSION

Curriculum writing teams often elect to develop supplemental resources for a theme study, beyond the essential concepts, guiding questions, content summaries, and performance assessments. For example, they may design graphic organizers for students that help to make clear the connections among ideas. Another valuable supplementary resource is a collection of ideas for activities communicated through published activity webs or organized activity sections of the resource book. Glossaries and bibliographies are often added to the Theme Resource Book.

Teacher-made materials and a variety of purchased materials complete the Theme Box.

The Theme Box is a complete resource unit prepared for implementing teachers. Chapter 9 explains the decisions that implementing teachers make as they design a teaching unit and implement the theme study in the classroom while using the Theme Box.

1. As a team, come to consensus on the most important information you want to communicate to students. Ask these questions:
   What is important for students to learn?
   What is of most interest to students?

2. Determine what type of graphic organizer best organizes this information. Ask the question:
   How can we present the information most effectively?

3. Complete a rough draft of the organizer with major points in relation to supporting information.

4. Determine what media will be used for the finished graphic organizer. For example: chart, overhead transparency, flannel graph set, game board, or interactive bulletin board.

1. Determine if important information from your theme can be organized using each type of graphic organizer.

   a. Classification—organizes information into categories to facilitate comparisons. Important information to be organized:

   b. Hierarchical—presents a main concept with ranks or levels of subconcepts. Important information to be organized:

   c. Conceptual—conveys information through a central idea supported by facts, characteristics, or examples that cannot be ranked in levels. Important information to be organized:

   d. Sequential—arranges events in a logical order. Important information to be organized:

   e. Cyclical—organizes information in a continuous sequence of events with no discernible beginning or end. Important information to be organized:

2. Select the most complete or most effective organizers and complete a rough draft with major points and related supporting information.

3. Determine what media will be used for the finished graphic organizer. Examples include a chart, an overhead transparency, a flannel graph set, a game board, or an interactive bulletin board.

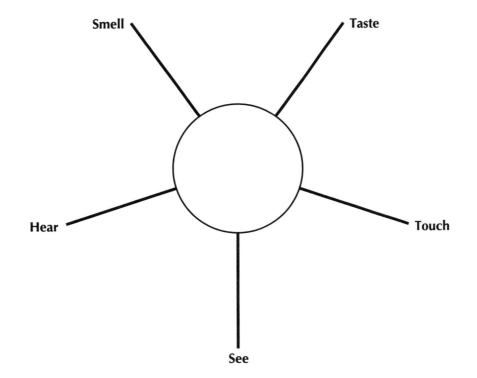

Instructions
1. Write theme focus in center hub.
2. List activity ideas by categories, following brainstorming rules.
3. Consciously search for ideas in each area.

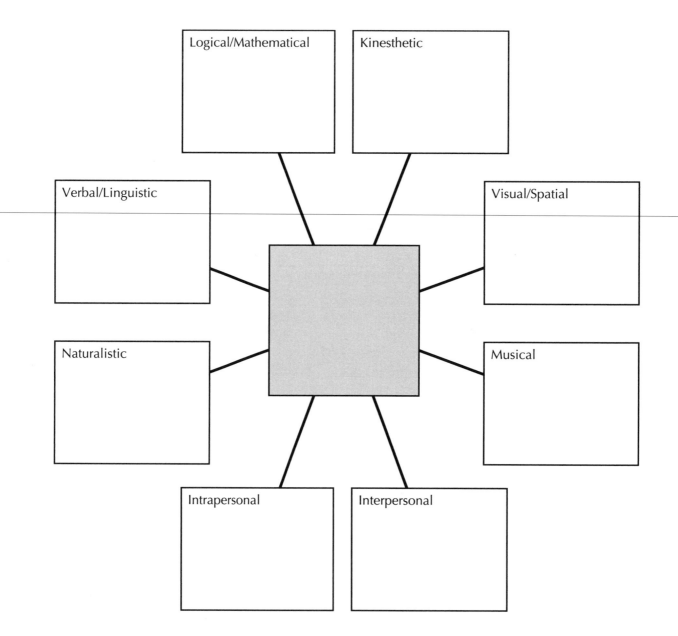

Logical/Mathematical

Kinesthetic

Verbal/Linguistic

Visual/Spatial

Naturalistic

Musical

Intrapersonal

Interpersonal

Instructions
1. Write theme focus in center hub.
2. List activity ideas by categories, following brainstorming rules.
3. Consciously search for ideas in each area.

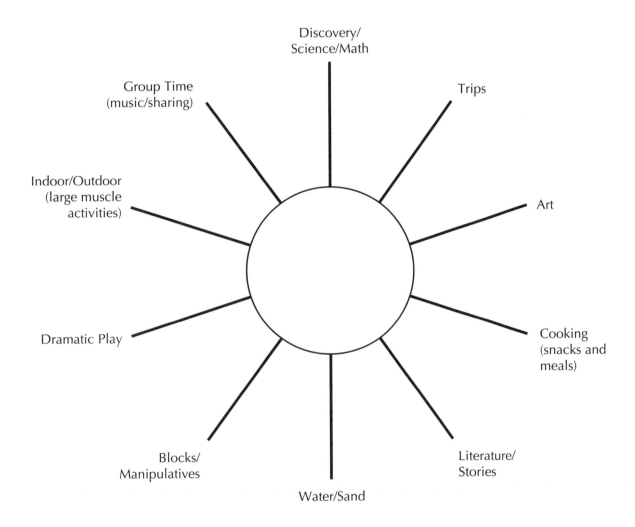

Instructions
1. Write theme focus in center hub.
2. List activity ideas by categories, following brainstorming rules.
3. Consciously search for ideas in each area.

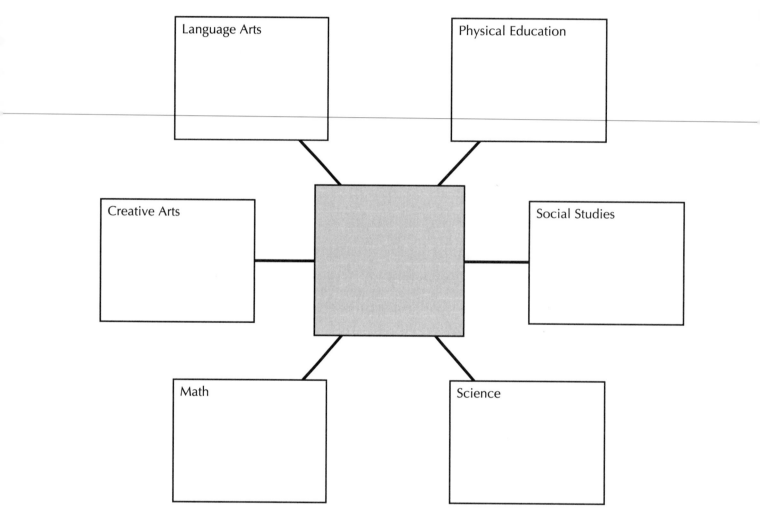

Language Arts

Physical Education

Creative Arts

Social Studies

Math

Science

Instructions
1. Write theme focus in center hub.
2. List activity ideas by categories, following brainstorming rules.
3. Consciously search for ideas in each area.

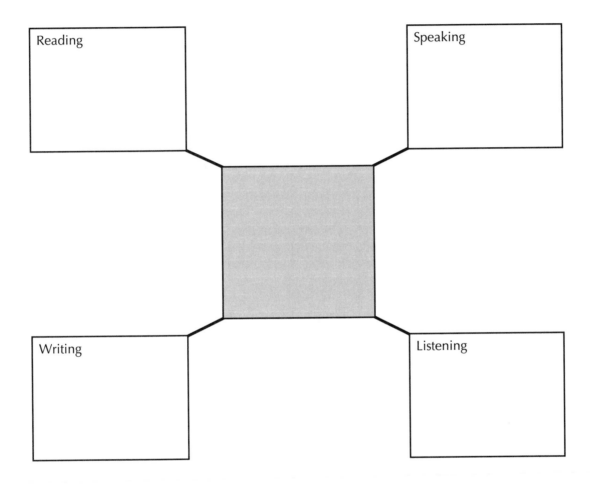

Reading

Speaking

Writing

Listening

Instructions
1. Write theme focus in center hub.
2. List activity ideas by categories, following brainstorming rules.
3. Consciously search for ideas in each area.

ACTIVITY PLANNING WEB—
INSTRUCTIONAL STRATEGIES

 **AP8-8**

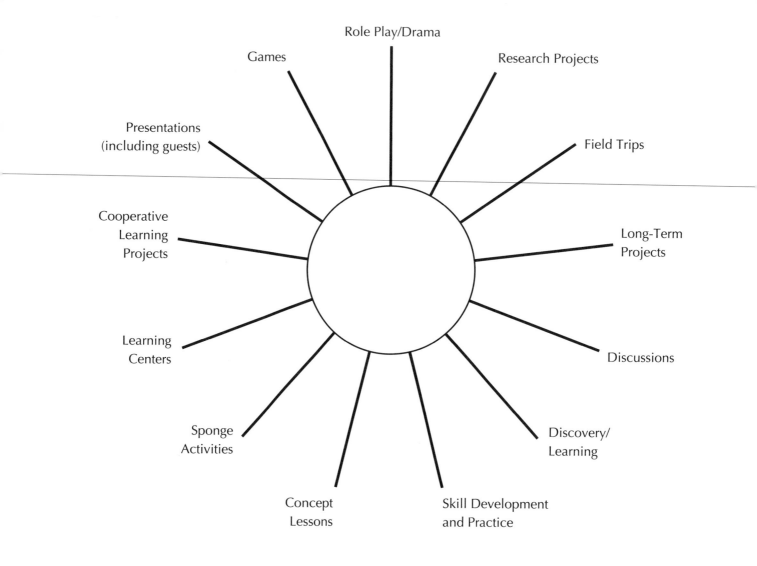

Role Play/Drama

Games

Research Projects

Presentations
(including guests)

Field Trips

Cooperative
Learning
Projects

Long-Term
Projects

Learning
Centers

Discussions

Sponge
Activities

Discovery/
Learning

Concept
Lessons

Skill Development
and Practice

Instructions
1. Write theme focus in center hub.
2. List activity ideas by categories, following brainstorming rules.
3. Consciously search for ideas in each area.

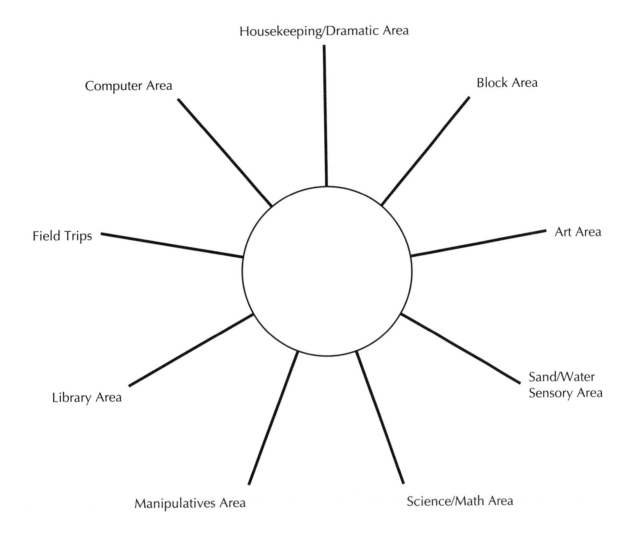

Housekeeping/Dramatic Area

Computer Area

Block Area

Field Trips

Art Area

Library Area

Sand/Water Sensory Area

Manipulatives Area

Science/Math Area

Instructions
1. Write theme focus in center hub.
2. List activity ideas by categories, following brainstorming rules.
3. Consciously search for ideas in each area.

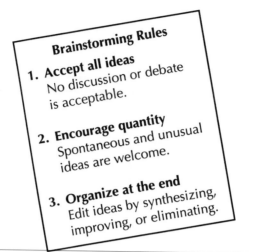

Brainstorming Rules

1. **Accept all ideas**
   No discussion or debate is acceptable.

2. **Encourage quantity**
   Spontaneous and unusual ideas are welcome.

3. **Organize at the end**
   Edit ideas by synthesizing, improving, or eliminating.

Instructions: As a team, review pieces of theme-related literature chosen for your Theme Box. Brainstorm possible activity ideas related to these books. You might want to consult the brainstorming planning webs on Action Packs 8-3 to 8-9 for categories to prompt your thinking. Record your brainstormed activities below.

Book (include all bibliographical data):

Brainstormed Activity Ideas:

Title: **Author:**

Illustrator: **Publisher & Date of Publication:**

Type of Book: **Grade/Age Level:**

Summary:

Notes on Illustrations:

Theme Connection:

Possible Respond Activities:

219

Step 1. Review activity ideas from several sources, including: published theme units, professional journals, teachers' manuals, Internet web sites, and other activity idea books. Using reviewed ideas or those provided on the next Action Pack pages, create three groups, representing poor, average, and excellent ideas.

Step 2. Using the group of excellent activities, analyze the characteristics that make these exceptional. List the criteria below.

Step 3. Using the group of poor activities, analyze what qualities these activities lack. List the criteria below.

Step 4. As a team, complete the criteria sections on the self-evaluation form on AP 8-13 and peer evaluation form on AP 8-14. Two critical criteria have been provided. Use the information from steps 2 and 3 above to complete your team's list of criteria.

Samples of Activity Ideas

Whales: Whale Endangerment

On a map, mark the countries that still kill whales today. Look at all of the countries that are marked and see where they are in relation to one another. Using the list of the species of whales killed and the number killed, find out how many whales are killed over a period of a specific number of years. Then discuss with the students if this would put any of these whales on the endangered species list. Find out why the students think they would be put there and ask them how they think this could be prevented.

Whales: Food Web

The students select a species of whale they would like to work on. Have the students write the name of their whale in the middle of the paper. The students should then draw sections and write the types of prey the chosen whale eats. This could also begin an activity that shows the ocean food chain, with the whale at the top. Students will show what they know about whales as they gain the knowledge that every animal has a place in a food chain.

Titanic: Create a Brochure

Create a brochure for the *Titanic* describing the rooms, the voyage, and any events the passengers can participate in while on the ship. Include pictures and details to describe everything. Remember to write like a salesperson, even about third-class rooms. Include sailing dates and also a price list. You may want to try creating this brochure for an invented ship called the *New Titanic,* instead.

Titanic: A Different Ending

Have the students rewrite the sinking of the *Titanic.* Leave this activity as open as possible. Students may choose to have the ship miss the iceberg, or have everyone be rescued after the hit. They may have everyone drown, or have the ocean liner run out of fuel, or . . . The possibilities are endless. You may want to encourage them to illustrate their stories, also, by drawing or using photographs.

Pittsburgh: Listening Walk

Listening walks are about being very quiet and noticing the sounds around you. There are a couple of children's books about this very idea that you can use to introduce it. Take students on a listening walk through your classroom, school building, and school grounds. Talk about and record different sounds they encountered on the walk. Make a tape of sounds of the city of Pittsburgh and play it for your class. Ask them to compare what they hear to what they heard on their listening walk at school. Make a class list or have students write journal entries.

Pittsburgh: 57 Varieties

Talk about Heinz's famous slogan "57 varieties." Create a math worksheet with math operations appropriate to the skill level of your students. Each problem should involve the number 57. You may want to put the math problems inside the shape of a ketchup bottle or pickle jar.

Pittsburgh: How Will We Travel?

This project can be a group activity or an individual activity. The children should be asked to tackle the question, "How will we travel in the future?" The children can answer by writing a description of a vehicle, the road system it will use, and the rules drivers will need to follow for safety. They can create a model or drawing of the vehicle. The students should use what they learned about transportation in Pittsburgh and be able to speak about the decisions they make.

Polar Animals: Egg Stand

Discuss with the students the way a penguin incubates its eggs. Divide the class into teams of two. Give each team a balloon filled with a small amount of water. Use just enough water to give the balloon weight. Then fill the balloon up with air. Have one team member stand with his feet together. Then place the balloon on top of one of that team member's feet. Have him stand there for three minutes before trying to pass it onto a partner's feet. Explain to the class that this is how a penguin cares for the egg. Impress on the students that it is very important to pass the egg gently without breaking it. Standing for three minutes seems like a long time to stand still. Ask the students how they would feel if they had to stand that way for several days.

Polar Animals: Over for Dinner

Students will act as if they are polar bears. They will each write a letter to another polar animal inviting it over for dinner. First each student must find out what the animal eats and then create a menu for dinner. Given several days, the children will research, write, and edit a menu for a polar bear guest.

National Parks: Writing Directions

Students can write directions about how to get from one national park to another. This would employ map and math skill. They can calculate the mileage and use a variety of different map reading skills. They would include the different states that they would travel through. If time permits, students could draw a map of the trip with the written directions on the bottom. You can challenge some students to draw the map to scale.

Fairy Tales: What Should Hansel Drop on the Trail?

Students are to determine which object would be best to drop on the trail as Hansel did in the story of *Hansel and Gretel*. Students have to take into consideration: What objects will blow away? Which objects would be affected by heat? Will animals eat or bother any of the choices? After they figure out which they believe to be the best object, have the class test their hypotheses on the school grounds.

Fairy Tales: Design an Invitation

Have the children pretend that they are the prince in *Cinderella* and design the invitation for the royal ball. What do they think that it would look like? Encourage the children to be as creative as possible, and to use correct spelling and grammar.

Fairy Tales: Growing Beans

This is an activity that can take place over several weeks. While reading the fairy tale *Jack and the Beanstalk*, the children can grow their own beans. They can fill plastic cups with potting soil, plant a seed, and water it. Over a period of time, they can keep track of the growth of their beans by measuring them and plotting their growth on a graph. The children can compare their beans and discuss the different parts of the plants.

Instructions: List additional team-generated criteria on the grid below.
After writing three activity descriptions, use this checklist to determine
if criteria are met.
Use a "+" to indicate the criteria that are the strengths of the activity.
Use an "×" to indicate the criteria that are present but are not strengths.
Use a "−" to indicate the criteria that are absent from the activity.

Criteria for Activities	Idea 1	Idea 2	Idea 3
1. Addresses concepts and guiding questions.			
2. Crosses discipline lines where appropriate.			
3.			
4.			
5.			
6.			
7.			
8.			
9.			
10.			

Instructions: When activity sections are completed, choose three ideas at random to spot-check. Attach a copy of the three activity ideas to this evaluation form. Use this checklist to determine if criteria are met.

Use a "+" to indicate the criteria that are the strengths of the activity.

Use an "×" to indicate the criteria that are present but are not strengths.

Use a "−" to indicate the criteria that are absent from the activity.

Criteria for Activities	Idea 1	Idea 2	Idea 3
1. Addresses concepts and guiding questions.			
2. Crosses discipline lines where appropriate.			
3.			
4.			
5.			
6.			
7.			
8.			
9.			
10.			

TEACHER-MADE MATERIALS DIRECTIONS  AP8-15

Theme:

Name of Creator:

Name of Creation:

Recommended Ages:

Purposes:

Materials Needed:

Directions for Making Material (if appropriate):

Directions for Using Material (if appropriate):

Possible Adaptations for Use of Material:

Note: Where appropriate, attach patterns to this page.

CRITERIA FOR TEACHER-MADE MATERIALS ■■■ AP8-16

Criteria	Ranking			
1. Attractive and visually stimulating	0	1	2	3
2. Versatile, allowing for adaptations	0	1	2	3
3. Related to theme concepts	0	1	2	3
4. Developmentally appropriate	0	1	2	3
5. Durable and safe	0	1	2	3
6. Simple in design	0	1	2	3
7. Material works as intended	0	1	2	3
8. Interactive and engaging for children	0	1	2	3
9. Precise, clear, complete directions	0	1	2	3

Scores:

0 - lacking
1 - needs revision
2 - acceptable
3 - excellent

CHAPTER 9

Implementing Theme Studies

GUIDING QUESTION

What are the Critical Decisions Teachers Must Make When They Implement a Theme Study?

Access to a Theme Box provides a classroom teacher with the tools to implement a theme study. She has the guidance of a team of teachers who have studied the content of the theme and created valuable resources. At the onset, she has the parameters for the study: a focus, concept statements, guiding questions for learners, a content summary, and performance assessments. The Theme Box also contains lists of locally available resources, some theme-related literature, and carefully selected teaching materials. However, implementing teachers must make many decisions when they develop a teaching unit and when they implement the theme study with a particular class.

WHAT ARE THE CRITICAL DECISIONS TEACHERS MUST MAKE WHEN THEY IMPLEMENT A THEME STUDY?

Teachers implementing a theme study will have a wide variety of decisions to make. Initial decisions revolve around the management of time and the amount of power to be shared with students. Teacher roles and student roles must be clarified. Implementing teachers also build a teaching unit by making decisions around initiating encounters, developing activities, and concluding activities. Finally, even when the study is complete, the teacher will make decisions when she reviews and evaluates the unit.

Decisions about Time

After studying the Theme Box contents and suggested resource materials, the implementing teacher's first decision relates to the pervasiveness of this theme study. This includes the determination of the overall theme study length as well as the necessary adjustments of the daily schedule required by the theme study. According to Walmsley (1996), a mini-theme would typically last one day in kindergarten and one week in sixth grade; an average theme would run one week in kindergarten and six weeks in sixth grade; and a major theme would last two weeks in kindergarten and twelve weeks in sixth grade. Jacobs (1991) suggests that themes typically run two to six weeks.

Themes are often shorter in the primary grades because individual research is limited by student capabilities, performance assessments are simpler, and content is less detailed. However, even in the primary years, a theme may spark an on-going interest that cannot easily be met in a one- or two-week time period.

A teacher must determine the schedule adjustments that would accommodate the subjects being integrated into the theme study. Schools using integrated curriculum vary tremendously in the amount of the school day that is integrated. Integration of the daily schedule includes options along a continuum ranging from a couple of hours a week to a completely integrated day as represented by Figure 9.1. At one end of the spectrum are schools or classrooms where teachers augment a more traditional curriculum with a couple of hours a week of interdisciplinary theme study. Often the theme focus coincides with the ongoing curriculum topics. At the other extreme are the schools using the integrated day model, with the entire curriculum based on themes, problems, and projects pursued in an interdisciplinary way. In these classrooms, the schedule is not divided along discipline lines in any way. Often the themes and projects pursued are selected from students' emerging interests. The integrated day approach is most common in early childhood settings where considerable academic freedom exists in curriculum decisions.

To make a decision about the portion of the daily schedule committed to the integrated theme study, a teacher needs to ask: What subjects can be meaningfully integrated into this theme study? Will these subjects also need additional time in the schedule to meet objectives? For example, while math can be integrated into many themes in a meaningful way, the time allocated and the range of content coverage may not be adequate to meet state requirements or student needs. In sample schedules provided by Jacob's (1989), about one-fifth of the available weekly time was allotted to theme work. Teachers at the Nova Scotia School (Gamberg, Kwak, Hutchings, & Altheim, 1988) generally allot

Figure 9.1 *Sample Integration Continuum*

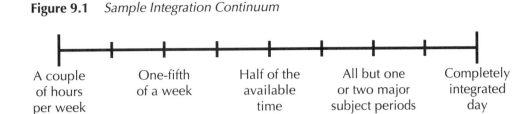

A couple of hours per week

One-fifth of a week

Half of the available time

All but one or two major subject periods

Completely integrated day

one-half of the scheduled time to theme studies. Many teaching teams and school-wide planning teams have started out by designing and implementing only one or two theme units a year and have gradually added more themes each year. Regardless of the amount of integrated curriculum time, any change toward integration requires a commitment of planning, time, and money.

Decisions about Control

Another preliminary decision facing the implementing teacher is how directive her teaching approach will be. Before starting the theme study, the teacher needs a clear vision of what roles will be assumed by teachers and by students. This primary and critical decision will influence every other decision made throughout the theme study. The range of possibilities is best represented on the continuum in Figure 9.2 with a prescriptive teacher-directed approach on one end and a student-directed approach on the other. In between are various degrees of shared power. A description of these three alternatives will illustrate possible options.

TEACHER-DIRECTED APPROACHES   When using a prescriptive teacher-directed approach, the teacher is the decision maker in all instances. He sees his role as managing all elements to achieve carefully established outcomes. He selects the themes to be studied; he sets all content goals and objectives; he designs all the content learning activities; and he determines the sequence and duration of the unit. Often the teacher prescribes the exact activities to achieve the established outcomes

Figure 9.2 *Sample Leadership Continuum*

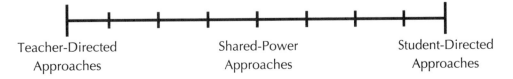

Teacher-Directed Approaches

Shared-Power Approaches

Student-Directed Approaches

without first having the opportunity to assess student needs and interests. During the teaching of the unit, the teacher presents a carefully and logically sequenced set of lessons and experiences to reach established goals. The teacher tests or assesses for mastery and, if needed, reteaches parts of the content. This prescriptive approach has two advantages. First, the teacher can fully prepare the unit before teaching it to the students. Second, the teacher has confidence that the content he values most will be addressed. However, with a detailed plan already constructed, the teacher encounters a major disadvantage: He cannot comfortably respond to the students' prior knowledge and changing needs and interests. The course has been predetermined.

STUDENT-DIRECTED APPROACHES   Student-directed approaches, at the other end of the continuum, empower the students as primary decision makers. In some student-centered programs, the learners' emerging interests determine what themes are studied. Student questions and interests determine the content as well as the sequence. With teacher guidance, students develop the plans for answering their own questions. Typically, most student-directed theme study development is done through independent or small-group investigation. Finally, the students decide when they are done with a theme study. Some teachers have the entire class vote on when it is ready to end a theme. Other teachers using a student-directed approach work more individually, encouraging a student or a small group to change direction when interests seem to be changing. Many teachers using this approach believe outcomes cannot be predicted in advance. Also, they believe outcomes for one learner are likely to be very different from those of another learner. Thus, they do not spend time identifying outcomes before beginning the study. Rather, the teachers ensure that student research activities and projects are holistic in nature, address the learners' own questions, and involve many areas of development.

The basic procedures for a student-directed approach are to involve students in making daily plans for their own learning and to engage students in researching their own questions under the guidance of the teachers. The teacher's role is to provide resources, provoke thinking, and support problem solving throughout the study. A minimum of direct teaching, direct information sharing, or direct skill modeling is done. As students execute their plans, they are encouraged to be as independent as possible. Teachers meet with the students regularly to assess their learning and provide support in problem solving. Additionally, students commonly share plans and new findings in group meetings.

One advantage of this approach is that students following their own interests are highly motivated and engaged. Furthermore, students are becoming independent learners and problem solvers. However, this approach has two major disadvantages. First, because teachers are severely limited in the advance preparation they can do, they must study, gather resources, and prepare as the theme progresses. A second major disadvantage is the doubtful quality of the questions guiding student investigations. Because student-generated questions are often very narrowly focused, the class may never reach an understanding of broader and more universal concepts and issues. Thus, investigations that are completely student-led may not lead to in-depth understanding of global concepts.

SHARED-POWER APPROACHES   The approach of most teachers implementing theme studies is somewhere between the two extremes of teacher-directed and student-directed alternatives. Teachers share control of the study with students. Teachers using a shared-power model believe that students can be trusted with many decisions and greatly benefit from having ownership in the study. Many teachers gradually relinquish decision-making opportunities as students appear ready to profit from the responsibility. On the other hand, teachers assert control by introducing profitable ways of learning and important content that would not occur to students. Teacher judgment as well as student interest is valued.

Teachers and students negotiate the curriculum in many ways. Teachers identify a theme focus, guiding questions, concepts worth understanding, and performance assessments. However, within these boundaries, student interests influence the specific emphases of the theme study. Implementing teachers and students work together to brainstorm questions to pursue and ways to learn. In a shared-power model, teachers strive to use a wide variety of instructional strategies, depending upon the identified outcomes. Independent research of the learner's own questions is typically one type of ongoing activity. Furthermore, in teacher-initiated activities or experiences, students are given a wide range of choices in issues such as topics, resources, and learning partners. Last, a combination of teacher judgment and sustained student interest determines the duration of the theme study. Figure 9.3 presents a comparison of the three approaches to thematic implementation. A detailed description of one model of a shared-power approach completes this chapter. This shared-power approach highlights the roles of implementing teachers and students in a negotiated curriculum.

Figure 9.3 *Comparison of Leadership Approaches*

	Teacher-Directed	Shared-Power	Student-Directed
Theme Choice	Teacher chooses theme	Student interests are a major concern in choosing theme	Student interests determine theme
Content and Objectives	Teacher determines content and objectives	Teacher's priorities and students' questions shape content and objectives	Students' questions determine content and objectives
Theme Duration	Teacher determines duration	Teacher judgment and sustained student interest influence duration	Students' continued interest determines duration
Determination of Outcomes	Outcomes are predetermined	Some outcomes are preset; others evolve	Outcomes are unpredictable
Instructional Strategies	Tendency toward deductive approaches	Wide variety of strategies used with emphasis on inductive approaches	Strong emphasis on independent inquiry

Decisions throughout the Shared-Power Stages

The shared-power model of implementing a negotiated theme study has six main stages:

1. Making advance preparations
2. Implementing initiating encounters
3. Building a teaching unit plan
4. Implementing developing activities
5. Concluding the theme study
6. Evaluating the theme study.

The implementing teachers will face a number of important decisions at each stage. These stages are summarized in Figure 9.4.

STAGE ONE: MAKING ADVANCE PREPARATIONS The implementing teacher begins advance preparations by studying the Theme Box resources and additional cited resources. In this way, the teacher gains background information on the focus content and understands ways of

Figure 9.4   *Six Stages of the Shared-Power Model*

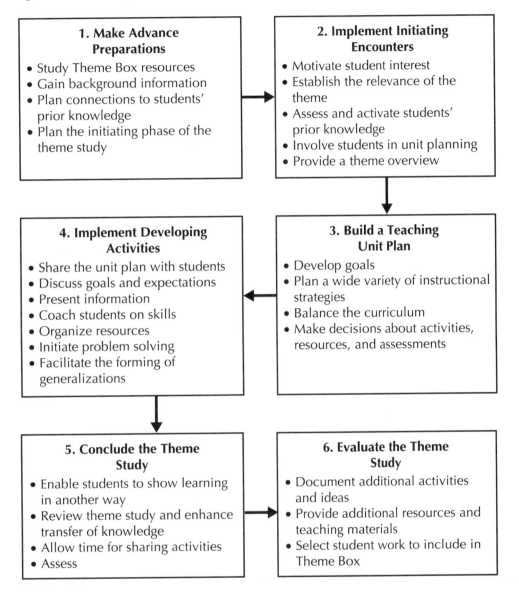

developing the chosen concepts. From the outset, the implementing teacher may decide to limit the theme study to only some of the concepts. Another part of advance preparation is gathering additional resources for student use. Also, the implementing teacher should determine ways to strengthen possible connections between the current theme study and past themes, areas of study, or experiences of students.

LINDA: *When I joined a second grade class as a student teacher and began preparing my thematic unit on the African grasslands, I noticed student-drawn pictures of endangered animals displayed in the classroom. Many of the depicted animals live in the grasslands. These pictures encouraged me to think about ways this previous work and other topics the students had studied related to the African grasslands. Suddenly, I saw connections to the children's prior learning everywhere. In language arts, they were reading fables and soon would be reading folktales, a related genre of literature. In science, students were in the middle of a thematic unit on weather and were tracking local weather. I saw ways they could apply this knowledge to a comparative study of weather and climate in the African grasslands. In social studies, the students were learning about buying and selling in different kinds of markets around the world, so we included a market-day activity in our theme study. By thinking about possible connections, I was able to plan activities that effectively built on the students' prior knowledge.*

Armed with a thorough study, many valuable resources, and ideas for strengthening connections, the teacher next lays careful plans for the initiating phase of the theme study. Once initiated, the rest of the unit will be planned with significant input from the students.

STAGE TWO: IMPLEMENTING INITIATING ENCOUNTERS   The launching of a theme study achieves many goals. The first goal is motivating interest. A captivating theme focus is not enough; the theme must be introduced in a motivating way that generates interest, questions, and curiosity. A goal closely tied to a motivating introduction is immediately establishing the theme relevance for students. For example, students who have never seen the ocean must come to understand the ways learning about it can matter to them. Thus, implementing teachers have the responsibility of leading learners to see both the importance and excitement of the theme in the initiation stage of the theme study.

Another crucial aspect of the initiating stage is assessing students' prior knowledge, their greatest interests relative to the theme focus, and their preferred ways of learning. While assessing and activating prior knowledge, teachers consider both the focus of the theme and background knowledge at a higher level of abstraction. For example, when implementing a theme on explorers of the past, present, and future, teachers would assess students' general notions about explorers. However, it would be equally important to assess their concepts of time. What is the past to them? Do they have a concept of time that allows them to discriminate a past of thirty years ago from a past of three hundred years ago? Likewise, teachers introducing the study of a geographic region such as the African grasslands would assess students' general notions of geography as well as their understanding of grasslands and Africa.

Another major goal of the initiating stage is involving students in unit planning and decision making. Teachers invite students to pose questions, make predictions, identify things to be learned, and suggest ways to learn them. All student ideas should be respectfully accepted, recorded, and in some way acted upon. A word of caution here: if student ideas are sought but not truly valued, students feel patronized and not powerful at all. Clearly, not all student ideas will be fully implemented, but their ideas should have a powerful influence on the final teaching plan.

An additional goal throughout the initiating stage is to provide an overview or big picture of the theme and the many possible ways to view it. The big picture is addressed in three ways. In some cases, the big picture is clarified through addressing ways this particular theme study connects to other themes previously studied. A second way to provide the big picture is by putting the theme focus into a larger context at a higher level of abstraction. A third way is to focus on the biggest ideas by introducing the guiding questions to the students.

Many types of activities are used to effectively initiate a theme study. These include: impression-making activities, brainstorming activities, assessment activities, multiple perspective activities, and big picture activities.

Impression-Making Activities. The goal of impression-making activities is to invite students into the theme study by quickly capturing their attention and interest in a compelling way. Teachers can make a theme engaging from the very beginning in numerous ways. A change in the physical learning environment is one approach. One teaching team put up a beautiful bulletin board of the rain forest. Without commenting on it to the students, they proceeded to dismantle parts day by day, symbolizing ongoing destruction. When the students began asking questions and making predictions about why their teachers were behaving so strangely, the teachers introduced the unit on the rain forests. Bulletin boards, activity centers, and room decorations are all changes signaling something new and exciting is about to begin. Special events such as field trips or guest speakers are typically scheduled near the end of a theme study, but they can be used instead as a motivating introduction. Dressing in costume or presenting a dramatization such as a skit or puppet show works well for some themes. One of our favorite impression-making activities is a Theme Box browse. Resource books, teacher-made materials, pictures, and artifacts from the Theme Box are spread throughout the room and learners are invited to browse through them. Teachers conduct no preliminary discussion of the theme. Following the browse, teachers can structure a discussion to elicit student reactions, questions, predictions, and stories about their personal experiences spawned by the Theme Box materials. Teachers of young children may need to give guidelines for careful handling of the learning materials by presenting Theme Boxes as treasure chests of valuable resources that must be treated respectfully.

Brainstorming Activities. A second type of valuable initiating activity is brainstorming. One brainstorming technique invites students to list all they know about a topic, then document the things they would like to find out. These are the beginning steps of the KWL charting strategy developed by Ogle (1986). *K* stands for: "What do you *know*?," *W* for "What do you *want* to know?," and *L* is presented at the unit's end when the chart is completed with "What have you *learned*?" An alternative brainstorming strategy is to ask students to list everything that comes to their minds when they think about the focus. For example, in a literature-based theme, after reading the focus piece of literature, students may make free associations about everything the story brought to mind. Collecting predictions is often an objective of brainstorming. For example, after a Theme Box browse, students might be asked questions such as: What do you think these materials are all about? What do you think we will be learning? What personal experiences did these materials bring to mind?

Regardless of the questions initiating brainstorming, many benefits can be expected. Brainstorming brings student attention to the theme study focus. Brainstorming enables the teacher to understand student ideas, attitudes, knowledge, and specific interests within the broad theme focus. Furthermore, it communicates to learners that their ideas are valued and respected and that they are expected to share the responsibility for this theme study. Finally, brainstorming communicates that risk taking is not only acceptable, but encouraged in theme studies.

Students need rules and procedures for brainstorming even when their brainstorming activity is teacher directed. Figure 9.5 gives an adaptation for students of the rules and procedures for brainstorming used throughout this book. To gain the greatest potential from brainstorming activities, everyone must participate. Therefore, the ideal

Figure 9.5   *Sample Brainstorming Rules for Students*

1. Everyone in the group shares one idea. After one go-around, you may either give an idea or pass.
2. All ideas are okay and are written down.
3. Your goal is to have lots of ideas.
4. Don't talk about any ideas until everybody has offered all of their ideas.
5. Set a time limit or turn limit on brainstorming.

arrangement is brainstorming within small groups of students. If this is not possible, the teacher may have students brainstorm independently first and then participate in the total group process.

Assessment Activities. Implementing teachers canvas learner needs, preferences, and current understandings in a variety of ways. Students might be interviewed by teachers or parent volunteers. Students could be asked to complete simple surveys addressing their attitudes or preferred learning styles. All this data is important to a teacher wanting student interests, preferences, and real questions to influence the curriculum. One way to determine high interest concepts is by clustering learners' questions and comments offered during brainstorming around the concepts identified by the curriculum team. Even voting can be used to determine student preferences.

> LINDA: *When introducing my unit on the African grasslands, my students browsed through materials from the Theme Box. The materials were grouped by concept. At each concept station, students voted on three activities from 8 or 9 options. My objective was to include one or two of the students' favorite activities to support each concept. To my surprise, 90 percent of the children chose learning Swahili words as one of their favorite activities. Instead of doing just one small activity around Swahili words, as I had originally intended, I added a Swahili word or phrase of the day to my unit plans. One student checked a Swahili-English dictionary out of the library so that the class could learn additional words of interest to them.*

Multiple Perspectives Activities. In an interdisciplinary theme, learners should be encouraged from the beginning to look at the theme focus from many perspectives. To accomplish this, ask students for their ideas about ways they could use each of their school subjects to help them learn about a theme. For example, a primary teacher implementing a dinosaur theme might ask: "How could we use what we know about writing to help us learn about dinosaurs? How could we use math? How can we use the scientific method?" An alternative approach, especially effective with older students, is inviting them to imagine they are different kinds of specialists. "If you were a scientist, what would you want to know about the desert? If you were a poet, what about the desert would interest you? What questions would you have about the desert if you were an historian?" This type of discussion helps students to realize the unique perspectives each discipline offers while enabling them to see ways the disciplines interconnect.

The Big Picture Activities. Activities enabling students to understand where the theme focus fits into a larger context can also be profitable at the beginning of the theme study. For example, if a piece of literature is used, the teacher may explore some unique features of the genre that selection represents. Alternatively it might be important to do a background study of the author. If the focus is a period in history such as Colonial America, some timeline work may give a broader perspective. If an abstract concept such as courage is studied, the teacher may wish to initially explore ways courage relates to character development. If the study focus is a geographic region such as the rain forest, the broader concept of geographic regions may require attention. When providing a larger context for a theme study, teachers often explore ways the current theme might connect to previous themes studied. Effective ways to introduce the guiding questions also fit into the category of big picture activities.

STAGE THREE: BUILDING A TEACHING UNIT PLAN   At this point, the teacher is ready to make many of the decisions and plans for the development of the teaching unit. The teacher now has a great deal of data about student experiences, concepts, misconceptions, and interests. The information derived from the initiating stage enables the teacher to make appropriate decisions about the unit plan. There are two important goals when designing units: variety and balance.

The implementing teacher will want to use a wide variety of instructional activities and strategies, including both teacher-initiated activities and student-initiated pursuits. Time must be allocated for skill coaching and vocabulary work. The teacher will most likely plan some presentations of information through guest speakers, field trips, media, and teacher presentations. Typically, teachers allocate a large block of time to student projects and research. Teachers using a shared power curriculum believe that in-depth understanding is constructed by students through holistic experiences and the active manipulation of materials and ideas. These learning encounters move more slowly than presentations and require teacher involvement as a facilitator and prompter.

Another goal in designing the teaching plan is focused on the balance issue. The implementing teacher will attempt to balance curricular areas being integrated. He will use a variety of types of grouping patterns including heterogeneous cooperative groups and shared interest groups. A balance of skill and process objectives needs to be identified. These include language skills, math skills, social skills, higher level thinking skills and research skills. Last, the teacher will want the theme study to use a variety of ways of learning and levels of understanding. Charting experiences by using Gardner's multiple intelligences (1993) or Bloom's taxonomy of cognitive, psychomotor, and affective objectives (1956) will help the teacher address this need for balance.

Unit plan design requires teachers to make decisions about several aspects: assessment, literature-based activities, human resources, research activity, long term projects, teacher initiated activities, and environment.

Decisions about Assessment. One of the first decisions an implementing teacher makes is determining the assessment activities. The Theme Box will provide suggestions for performance assessments. The implementing teacher is now in an excellent position to select or adapt a performance assessment task or project suggested by the curriculum team. This decision should not be delayed. Most performance assessments require significant time and in some cases take over the direction of the theme study. The implementing teacher considers other assessment options such as the use of portfolios, journals, research reports, interviews, and anecdotal records. As teachers plan strategies for careful documentation of the learning that occurs, they are making later theme evaluation possible. Pictures can be taken, brainstorming charts saved, processfolios maintained, student products saved, and notes collected on teacher insights.

Decisions about Literature-Based Activities. Theme-related literature will allow students to view the focus from several perspectives. The literature in the Theme Box is chosen because of its quality and potential for teaching the chosen concepts. Teachers may opt to use literature as part of the available resources for research, to read aloud one or more selections, or to assign independent reading of some selections. If the Theme Box contains sets of books, implementing teachers might establish student reading groups. Each group might read and discuss one book and then plan responses to share with the whole class. Students engaged in this option will need quiet reading time early in the theme study, followed by small group time later. An alternative strategy to use late in the theme study is that of book sharing groups. This strategy requires that each student has read a different book. As students teach each other about their books, they can draw comparisons about the information and perspectives on the total collection of books.

Decisions about Research Activity. Decisions about individual and group research activities affect how students will pursue their own questions and pose additional questions. Researching with partners or in groups of three has several advantages for learners. In small groups, students learn from each other and support each other while learning important social skills. If groups larger than three or four are used, teachers frequently see some students passively viewing the activity. Furthermore, teachers often prefer group research because they have fewer projects to track. When creating research groups, teachers should consider not only shared interests but varied learning styles and strengths.

Decisions about Long-Term Projects. In addition to performance assessment projects and research projects, other long-term projects might be planned. Plans may need to be made for flowers or vegetables to be planted, butterfly observation centers to be established, eggs to be hatched, community interviews to be scheduled, or a play to be produced.

Decisions about Teacher-Initiated Activities. Teachers may want to plan some short-term teacher-initiated experiences. Planning all of these activities is not necessary, or even desirable. Indeed, the need for many of these interventions will result from outcomes that cannot be anticipated. However, the teacher will want to schedule those few teacher-initiated activities having the greatest potential for focusing on the chosen concepts, skill and process goals, and expressed student interests.

Decisions about Human Resources. Implementing teachers need to identify and communicate early with the human resources involved in the theme study. Thus, the involvement of subject-matter experts can be carefully planned and comfortably scheduled. The students' families should be high on this resource list. Theme studies are an excellent and meaningful place for parent or family involvement. Families can help identify artifacts related to the theme content as well as help to provide project materials. Long-term projects and field trips benefit from extra family help. Furthermore, family members may have expertise that would be a great asset to the study.

Decisions about Environment. Implementing teachers should thoughtfully plan learning centers, classroom environments, and extended learning environments. Elementary and middle school teachers know well the power of the physical environment to communicate. Classrooms, students' homes, and the community can all send the message that these are places to observe, create, question, try out, read, consult, and write. The first consideration is the classroom itself. Every area of the classroom can become a tantalizing invitation to learn about the theme. Moreover, every area should clearly indicate the type of work to be conducted there and should be well equipped and organized, providing the needed learning tools. Teachers give consideration to decorations, bulletin boards, posters, murals, and mobiles. Theme-related games, music, musical instruments, books, puppets, costumes, and manipulatives might be added to learning centers. As time allows, students can help transform the room.

When thinking about environmental decisions, teachers often find ways to extend the theme study into the students' homes through appropriate and creative assignments requiring home resources. For example, many homes have computers with interactive encyclopedias and Internet connections, allowing students to do research at home. Parents and other family members can themselves be valuable resources as they assist with projects or share their knowledge and expertise. Many theme studies have natural connections to community resources as well.

> LINDA: *When doing a minitheme on the Winter Olympics with kindergarten children, I reviewed with children the television schedule each day to find events that would be on during the early evening. Each evening the students had a short viewing assignment, bringing back information for the next day's class discussion. In addition, I would videotape short segments of events occurring after the children's bedtimes to show during our Olympics moments. The students followed the Olympics closely, chose favorite sports and athletes, and tracked the number of medals won. Several students brought magazine and newspaper articles to share with the class. Some parents shared that their children chose to watch the Olympic games rather than their favorite television programs.*

STAGE FOUR: IMPLEMENTING DEVELOPING ACTIVITIES Once the teacher develops the teaching unit plan, she should share it in an age appropriate way with the learners. The students need the opportunity to discuss with the teacher ways they will be learning and expectations these approaches imply. While it would be a mistake to overwhelm students with all the details of unit plans, the classroom teacher can give them an overview of the organization of their work. In areas where the teacher is willing to adjust, she can ask students for refinements and modifications to the teaching plan. Once again, the teacher is advised to solicit feedback only on decisions she is willing to negotiate. Otherwise, she should simply communicate her decisions. Although broad concepts, performance assessments, and time constraints may all be decisions that are not negotiated, other decisions can be negotiated as time allows.

Teacher Roles throughout the Development Stage. Anytime a teacher uses a wide variety of instructional strategies, her role will change from activity to activity. Sometimes she will present information. Other times she will demonstrate procedures or skills and then coach learners in attempting them. Clearly, a teacher of themes must organize all kinds of resources for learning. Many times the teacher serves as a catalyst for problem solving, giving students a helpful structure for group work. However, the one thing the teacher can never afford to be is uninvolved. The belief that teachers can get good results merely from getting out of learners' way and letting them "do their own thing" is an outdated notion. Significance is made by the students and teachers working together, not by students struggling on their own to investigate. Teachers are needed to help students formulate generalizations and to identify the important patterns that emerge from their research. Two types of strategies that exemplify this type of teacher involvement are process discussions and content discussions.

Teachers can focus student attention on important thinking processes, feelings, and social processes through total group or small group discussions on process issues. Questions to ask students might include: How did you begin to find answers to your research questions? How did you know when a book was right for you? What were some really tough parts of this project? What did you do when you came to a tough part? Did it work? What worked well for your group? What did you do in this research project that you could do at home if you were curious about something else? What strategies did you hear about in your group today that you could use in your own work? How did your partner help you with this project? How could you have worked better together? As you discuss process issues with students, ask many questions related to the process of investigating ideas. Teacher-led discussions encourage students to understand the significance and potential applications of their own thinking processes and problem solving strategies. Also, some questions should focus on the process of working effectively with classmates. Growing in the interpersonal skills of team work and cooperation takes time, effort, discussions, and strategies. Furthermore, some questions should focus on the feelings, attitudes, and values that have an important place in theme studies affecting learners' lives.

DOROTHY: *While I was attending a conference on Constructivism, I happened to sit beside a gentleman preparing to retire from a career as a psychologist and counselor. As we chatted before the session started, he shared with me his view that his life work had been about a search for the right questions to ask people. He freely shared with me seven key questions that he found to be effective when talking with others about their feelings. These questions seem promising in talking with students about their feelings regarding their learning experiences. They are:*

Do you ever feel (confused, proud, angry, frustrated, anxious)?
When?
Why then?
What do you do about that feeling?

Why is that what you do?

How does that work for you?

Is that what you want?

Teachers conduct discussions around content as well as process. As students engage in experiences and investigations, they individually construct an understanding of important ideas that could not be reached through direct presentations. However, teachers can greatly facilitate successful learning by posing leading or provocative questions: What have you learned that seems important to you? Why is this information important? What are the "biggest ideas" here? How did you come to that idea? How are Mike's ideas like Alicia's? How are they different? What do you think of that? What questions does that comparison suggest? What do you think someone who really wants to understand this topic should know? Why do you believe this to be so? Have you changed your mind about some things since studying this theme? The goal of these discussions is to help students formulate generalizations through inductive reasoning. With the teacher's help, learners move from their specific research information to broader concepts and generalizations. At the discussion's end, a teacher should summarize what the group has discovered together.

Another likely outcome of the discussion will be new questions. The class can document and research these questions as time permits. The collection of questions should be an ongoing classroom activity for individual students and groups. A good sign is when the list of questions about a theme focus is outgrowing the class time allocated to researching answers. Mirroring real life, this communicates to students that their interest and curiosity in this topic need not end. In all likelihood, the class will revisit this theme in the months ahead as students and teachers discover new information or gain related experiences. As teachers work conscientiously to help students formulate effective questions, the level of student thinking will rise. Thoughtful questions can invite creativity, multiple answers, substantiated opinions, and logical analysis.

Student Roles throughout the Development Stage. If students are to do more than collect pieces of factual information, they will need to fill roles related to recording data accurately, comparing information from multiple sources, organizing information, identifying patterns, and formulating new questions. Therefore, teachers using independent or small group research will need to teach strategies such as note taking, summarizing, and using graphic organizers. Students will also learn to use drawings, illustrations, and models as effective tools for organizing information.

One important goal for students at this stage is the independent use of organizing strategies to communicate their own understandings. The several steps in Figure 9.6 will help students learn to create graphic organizers, one type of organizing tool.

Step 1. Provide students with many examples of organizers that you have designed or taken from resources. Make sure the examples focus on the theme study content.

Step 2. Involve the students in discussing the organizers and analyzing their effectiveness. Consider doing "think alouds" (Davey, 1983) with the students by verbalizing your reasons for organizing the material as you did.

Step 3. Begin assisting students in the development of organizers by using partially completed ones, especially interactive organizers. Provide practice completing the organizers as a guided group activity. Again, use organizers focused on content relevant to your theme study. In this way, students are learning not only a strategy, but the interplay of ideas related to the theme.

Step 4. Have students work independently to finish partially completed organizers.

Step 5. Give students blank organizers that provide only the structure for organizing ideas. Provide guided practice for a variety of organizer types, highlighting the unique advantages of each type.

Figure 9.6   *Steps to Help Students Create and Use Graphic Organizers*

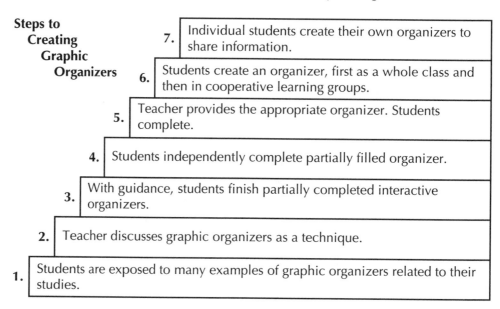

Steps to Creating Graphic Organizers

7. Individual students create their own organizers to share information.

6. Students create an organizer, first as a whole class and then in cooperative learning groups.

5. Teacher provides the appropriate organizer. Students complete.

4. Students independently complete partially filled organizer.

3. With guidance, students finish partially completed interactive organizers.

2. Teacher discusses graphic organizers as a technique.

1. Students are exposed to many examples of graphic organizers related to their studies.

Step 6. Have students decide on the type of organizer to use when summarizing different kinds of information. Do this first as a total class activity and then in cooperative learning groups.

Step 7. Have students design organizers to communicate information gathered in their own inquires.

As students are engaged in inquiry through theme studies, they should discover patterns and connections between ideas. They must distinguish major ideas from supporting ideas as they explain these connections among concepts. Graphic organizers, outlines, note cards, and models are tools for helping them learn to research.

STAGE FIVE: CONCLUDING THE THEME STUDY Many goals are achieved by the closing stage of a theme study. Certainly, one major goal is to assess the understanding of the big ideas or major concepts. Also, teachers want to enhance the transfer of both content understanding and process strategies that were learned during the theme study. Connections to other themes and other life issues should be established. Moreover, this is a time for students to celebrate and share with others what they have learned. Below are some culminating activity options to accomplish these goals.

Showing Learning Another Way. One of the best ways to strengthen and deepen what students have learned in a theme study is to invite them to show what they have learned in "another way." If students enjoy writing and have written research reports or a learning journal during the development stage, they can share what they know in a different genre such as poetry or a story. Students could show what they have learned through the creative arts: music, theater, dance, or drawing. Some students could plan a lesson for younger children to teach them about the theme focus. Often the chosen performance assessment does exactly this: it asks students to synthesize what they have learned to create a new product or performance.

The Theme Study in Review. Throughout the theme study, the implementing teacher carefully records the experiences and significant learnings of students through a variety of documents. The collection of theme study documents might include brainstorming webs, list of predictions, KWL charts, videos, photographs, drawings, graphic organizers, slides, student learning journals, and samples of work. In effect, this documentation becomes the class processfolio for the theme study. This documentation has great value in depicting a journey that can be studied, analyzed, and remembered in a meaningful way. A thoughtful documentation also invites students to revisit what has been studied and motivates their interest in continuing research of some areas.

The teacher should set aside time at the theme study conclusion to review and discuss the theme study documents. KWL charts and prediction lists could be completed. In addition, students may want to organize some types of documentation into more permanent exhibits. Slides might be organized into a scripted presentation; selected pictures might be enlarged or put into a scrapbook. The class might publish a web page on the theme. Some students might be able to edit a video to be circulated to students' homes. Once these activities are complete, generate with the students a list of unanswered questions that they may want to investigate independently. Finally, authorize students to select samples of student work to add to the school's Theme Box.

Sharing Activities. For many themes, students will want to share with others what they have learned. This may take the form of an open-house celebration for families, an exhibition for other classes in the school, or a one-on-one teaching experience with a younger student. Occasionally, these sharing activities are conducted on a grand scale with the whole community involved, but such events are not always necessary. Elaborate culminating events require a great deal of time and energy on the students' and teachers' parts. Teachers must give prudent consideration to whether the gains warrant these expenditures. Often a simpler sharing experience serves equally well.

Assessment Activities. This model of theme development has presented assessment as guiding instruction and enabling students to show what they are learning throughout the theme study. Therefore, it is an ongoing activity. However, some special assessment activities are needed for the closing stage. These may include completing performance assessments, entering portfolio documents, completing attitude surveys, and taking formal tests on the content studied.

STAGE SIX: EVALUATING THE THEME STUDY Teachers should reflect upon and evaluate the theme study at the conclusion of the unit. This should be done shortly after the theme study is concluded and before impressions, conclusions, and thoughts are lost. Including this evaluation in the Theme Resource Box provides the next teacher using that box with valuable information to guide the development of another teaching plan. Teacher evaluation should focus on the parameters of the study as well as the activities and resources. A natural outcome of teaching a theme is discovering many activity ideas, community resources, and teaching materials in addition to those originally provided in the Theme Box by the curriculum team. These should be gathered and added to the Theme Resource Box. Likewise, outdated or damaged materials should be removed. In addition, teachers should select student work samples to include in the Theme Box.

CONCLUSION

Classroom teachers build on the work of the school-based curriculum team by writing and implementing teaching plans for the theme study. Each teaching plan addresses the parameters of the theme study in a way uniquely suited to the needs, interests, and background knowledge of a particular class of students. Classroom teachers make several critical decisions about the theme study that impact the teaching plan, including time management, shared control of the curriculum with students, assessment decisions, resource decisions, and activity decisions. The work of the implementing teacher progresses through identifiable stages: (1) making advance preparations, (2) implementing initiating encounters, (3) building a teaching plan, (4) implementing developing activities, (5) concluding the theme study, and (6) evaluating the theme study.

During the evaluating stage, implementing teachers share information with the original curriculum writing team so that additions, updates, and adjustments may be made to the Theme Box. Through this evaluation and reflection process the Theme Box becomes a living resource for future teachers.

Bibliography

Aardema, Verna. (1977). *Who's in Rabbit's house?* New York: Dial Press.

Allen, D., & Piersma, M. (1995). *Developing thematic units: Process and product.* Albany, NY: Delmar Publishers.

ASCD. (1997). *Planning integrated units: A concept-based approach* (videotape). Alexandria, VA: Association for Supervision and Curriculum Development.

Berlin, D. F., & Hillen, J. A. (1994). Making connections in math and science: Identifying student outcomes. *School Science and Mathematics, 94,* 283–290.

Bloom, B. S. (Ed.). (1956). *Taxonomy of educational objectives. Handbook 1: Cognitive domain.* New York: David McKay.

Caine, R., & Caine, G. (1991). *Making connections: Teaching and the human brain.* Alexandria, VA: Association for Supervision and Curriculum Development.

Ceperley, P. (1991). Site-based decisionmaking: Policymakers can support it or undermine it. *The Link, 10*(2), 1, 7–9.

Cromwell, S. (1989). A new way of thinking: The challenge of the future. *Educational Leadership, 49*(1), 60–64.

Davey, B. (1983). Think aloud: Modeling the cognitive process of reading comprehension. *Journal of Reading, 27*(1), 44–47.

Davis, A. P., & Selvidge, M. J. (1995). *Focus on women.* Huntington Beach, CA: Teachers Created Materials, Inc.

dePaola, Tomie. (1975). *The cloud book.* New York: Holiday Publishing.

Dewey, J. (1916). *Democracy and education.* New York: Macmillan.

Dewey, J. (1938). *Experience and education.* New York: Macmillan.

Drake, S. M. (1993). *Planning integrated curriculum: The call to adventure.* Alexandria, VA: Association for Supervisor and Curriculum Development.

Fredericks, A. D., Meinbach, A. M., & Rothlein, L. (1993). *Thematic units: An integrated approach to teaching science and social studies.* New York: HarperCollins College Publications.

Friend, H. (1984). *The effect of science and mathematics integration on selected seventh grade students' attitudes toward and achievement in science.* New York: City Board of Education.

Gamberg, R., Kwak, W., Hutchings, M., & Altheim, J. (1988). *Learning and loving it.* Portsmouth, NH: Heinemann.

Gardner, H. (1983) *Frames of mind.* New York: Basic Books.

Gardner, H. (1993). *Multiple intelligences: The theory in practice.* New York: Basic Books.

Hergenhahn, B. R., & Olson, Matthew H. (1997). *An Introduction to theories of learning* (5th Ed.). Saddle River, NJ: Prentice Hall.

Hunter, M. (1994). *Enhancing Teaching.* New York: Macmillan.

Jacobs, H. H. (Ed.). (1989). *Interdisciplinary curriculum: Design and implementation.* Alexandria, VA: Association for Supervision and Curriculum Development.

Jacobs, H. H. (1991). Planning for curriculum integration. *Educational Leadership, 49,* 27–28.

Jacobs, H. H. (1997). *Mapping the big picture.* Alexandria, VA: Association for Supervision and Curriculum Development.

Johnson, R., Rynders, J., Johnson, D. W., Schmidt, B., & Haider, S. (1979). Interaction between handicapped and nonhandicapped teenagers as a function of situational goal structuring: Implications for mainstreaming. *American Educational Research Journal, 16,* 161–167.

Johnston, G. S., & Germinario, V. (1985). Relationship between teacher decisional status and loyalty. *The Journal of Educational Administration, 23*(1), 91–105.

Lionni, L. (1973). *Frederick.* New York: Knopf.

Lounsbury, J. H. (Ed.). (1992). *Connecting the curriculum through interdisciplinary instruction.* Columbus, OH: National Middle School Association.

Lowry, L. (1990). *Number the stars.* Boston: Houghton Mifflin.

MacIver, D. (1990). Meeting the need of young adolescents: Advisory groups, interdisciplinary teaching teams, and school transition programs. *Phi Delta Kappan 71*(6), 458–465.

Mansfield, B. (1989). Students' perceptions of an integrated unit: A case study. *Social Studies, 80*(4), 135–140.

McIntire, R. G., & Fessenden, J. F. (1994). *The self-directed school: Empowering the stakeholders.* New York: Scholastic.

Mohrman, S. A., Wohlstetter, P. et al. (1994). *School-based management: Organizing for high performance.* San Francisco: Jossey-Bass.

Ogle, D. (1986). K-W-L: A teaching model that develops active reading of expository text. *The Reading Teacher, 39,* 564–570.

Olarewaju, A. O. (1988). Instructional objectives: What effects do they have on students' attitudes towards integrated science? *Journal of Research in Science Teaching, 15*(4), 283–291.

Paterson, K. (1991). *Lyddie.* New York: Dutton Children's Books.

Piaget, J. (1954). *The construction of reality in the child.* New York: Basic Books.

Piaget, J. (1963). *Psychology of intelligences.* Paterson, NJ: Littlefield Adams.

Post, T. R., Ellis, A. K., Humphreys, A. H., & Buggey, L. J. (1997). *Interdisciplinary approaches to curriculum: Themes for teaching.* Upper Saddle River, NJ: Prentice Hall.

Schell, J. W., & Wicklein, R. C. (1993). Integration of mathematics, science, and technology education: A basis for thinking and problem solving. *Journal of Vocational Educational Research, 18,* 49–76.

Sharan, S., Kussell, P., Hertz-Lazarowitz, R., Bejarano, Y., Raviv, S., & Sharan, Y. (1984). *Cooperative learning in the classroom: Research in desegregated schools.* Hillsdale, NJ: Erlbaum.

Slavin, R. (1986). *Student team learning* (3d ed.). Baltimore, MD: Center for Research on Elementary and Middle Schools, Johns Hopkins University.

Slavin, R. (1995). *Cooperative learning* (2d ed.) Boston, MA: Allyn and Bacon.

Thompson, G. (1991). *Teaching through themes.* New York: Scholastic Professional Books.

Traver, R. (1998). What is a good guiding question? *Educational Leadership, 55*(6), 70–73.

Vygotsky, L. S. (1962). *Thought and language.* Cambridge, MA: MIT Press.

Vygotsky, L. S. (1978). *Mind in society.* Cambridge, MA: MIT Press.

Walmsley, S. A. (1996). Ten ways to improve your theme teaching. *Instructor,* 54–60.

Wasserstein, P. (1995). What middle schoolers say about their schoolwork. *Educational Leadership, 53*(1), 41–43.

Index